The Ultimate Roadtrip, A Guide to Leading Small Groups

Published by:

CruPress
CruPress is the publishing division of the Campus Ministry.

Campus Crusade for Christ
100 Lake Hart Drive 2500
Orlando, FL 32832

Cover and Book Design
Mark Arnold
andArnold.com

First Edition
©1995, WSN Press, Campus Crusade for Christ,
Inc. Orlando, FL

Second and Third Edition
©2005 ©2008, CruPress, Campus Crusade for
Christ, Inc. Orlando, FL

To Order go to
www.CruPress.com
Or call 1.800.827–2788

ISBN 1–56399–249–3

THE
ULTIMATE
ROAD
TRIP
A GUIDE TO LEADING
SMALL
GROUPS

crupress

The Publishing Division of the Campus Ministry
Campus Crusade for Christ

TABLE OF CONTENTS

ACKNOWLEDGEMENTS

(FIRST ADDITION, 1995)

This book was written by a small group of sorts, men and women who've led hundreds of groups in Campus Crusade for Christ over the past several decades. As in all small groups, each person made an invaluable contribution toward the final product and, as a result, this book is far better than if one person wrote it alone. The first group of writers met in Fort Collins, Colo., the summer of 1993. Ned Mervich, Dianne Henschel, Peggy Linn, Kelli Cox, Dennis Brockman and I spent several weeks forging the initial content for this project.

During the following school year, Kelli Cox, Gordon Klenck, Marajen Denman, Liz Swanson and Kent Mulkey added great stories and perspective, slowly building on the work from the previous summer. In April, the project was greatly helped by a brainstorming session at the Communication Center—thanks Tim, Glenn and Kent. Along the way Kelli became a mom and gave attention to her new son. Thank you, Kelli, for keeping this book afloat with your persistence and attention to detail.

Over the 1994–1995 school year, Dave Carlson, Judy-Clark and I wrote new chapters, rewrote old chapters, and polished up the manuscript. As we finalized each chapter, a group of veteran Campus Crusade staff members gave us their input. Their insightful critiques and contributions made the material much better. We're grateful to Jane Armstrong, Steve Pogue, Gladys Hillman, Ned Mervich, Eric and Liz Swanson, Ray and Diana Anderson, and Cynthia Hagen for their help. Gary Purdy and Marajen Denman went the extra mile, bailing us out on short notice by adding their multiple insights and talents.

As each chapter approached its final form, Greg Kriefall did a masterful job of editing confusing pronouns and rambling sentences. Barry Rush and Dennis Brockman gave leadership and direction to the overall development and production process. And Larry Thompson, Sherry Thompson and Laura Stowers of Thompson & Thompson Graphic Design did their usual expert job with the layout and graphics.

Over the past year Dave Carlson has been a constant companion via e-mail, telephone, face-to-face interaction, and express mail. Dave pored over this book numerous times, and the project is far better due to his talents and tireless work. Dave: thanks for your hard work, flexibility and creative brilliance. It's been a joy working with you.

Finally, I'd like to thank the people in my life who have sacrificed for this project—my wife and best friend, Sonya, and my children, Andrew and Meagan. Countless times they've wondered when Daddy would get off the computer. Many commited people have given financially to make our work possible. I want to thank everyone who cares enough to give financially to the great cause of reaching college students for Christ.

To God be all glory! The Holy One shares His glory with no one, and it is because of His grace and for His glory that we humbly offer this work to His world.

RICK HOVE

Libertyville, Illinois
Easter, 1995

PREFACE

The Ultimate Road Trip, Leading A Small Group. It isn't a title you would expect for a book on leading small groups, but then again this isn't your ordinary, run-of-the-mill book.

We like the road trip metaphor because it fits small groups. Groups, like road trips, have noteworthy destinations. And, like road trips, small groups are rich with relationships and good times. You need a great destination and relationships for a good trip and for a good small group.

Before we wrote a word for this book, we read. We devoured book after book, asking ourselves if anything new could be said about leading small groups. We concluded we could make a unique contribution to the vast resources available on small groups.

We envisioned a book that captured the thrill and power of small groups: the friendships and memories, the fun, the trials, the impact. This book would be fun to read, easy to learn from, and practical. And we wanted a book which would somehow contribute to God's kingdom, for He is the ultimate reason any of us even care about a book on small groups. You now hold our best effort.

All who contributed to the book have served Christ within the organization of Campus Crusade for Christ. The book reflects our experiences, values, and convictions, but the principles taught in it are not limited to Campus Crusade small group leaders.

Like every book, we had to leave some things out. This is a book about leading small groups. We haven't discussed what kind of group you might lead (evangelistic, cell, discipleship, or whatever), who should be in your group, how long you should meet, or the content you should discuss or teach. Those decisions are up to you.

This book is about *how* to lead a small group. And we think you'll likely find what you need to know about leading a group in these pages.

PREFACE TO THE THIRD EDITION

In the last decade The Ultimate Roadtrip has been read and reread by Bible study leaders all over the country, providing them with practical wisdom, time-tested ministry experience, and substantial theological insight. This third edition preserves all of the material of the second edition with the exception of reshuffling chapters five through eight, reformatting the questions in what is now chapter eight, and supplementing content in chapter five on what it means to change at the heart level. All other editorial changes are minor and for the most part unnoticeable.

Special thanks to Jeff Lark for providing additional content and editorial labor, and to Mark Arnold for his update and redesign of the book.

We trust that The Ultimate Roadtrip will continue to be a faithful guide and companion to Bible study leaders within the ministry of Campus Crusade and beyond.

RICK JAMES

Publisher, CruPress

Spring, 2008

WEST TEXAS

"WHERE THE DEER AND THE ANTELOPE PLAYED — WITH THE COMANCHES RIGHT BEHIND."

CHICAGO
ILLINOIS

© CURT TEICH & CO., INC.

GREETINGS FROM
DETROIT
MICHIGAN

600

Greetings from
PITTSBURGH
PENNA.

© C. T. & CO.

Greetings from
RENO
NEVADA

CURT TEICH & CO., INC.

Greetings from Glamorous HOLLYWOOD

THE ULTIMATE ROADTRIP

Greetings from
MISSOURI

Greetings from NORTH CAROLINA

Houston, Texas

87 USA

Greetings FROM HAWAII

IT'S M

IT ISN'T WHAT IT APPEARS TO BE.

1

LEADING A SMALL GROUP IS A GREAT ADVENTURE.

IT STARTS SMALL— BROWNIES AND STUFF.
BUT AS GOD CHANGES YOU AND WORKS IN YOUR GROUP, IT
BECOMES BIG, AS IN ETERNALLY BIG. IN FACT,
YOUR SMALL GROUP CAN BE THE VEHICLE
GOD USES TO CHANGE LIVES.

MORE.

WELCOME TO THE JOURNEY

1.1

THE ADVENTURE

Rarely do we stop to think of the influence a small group can have on its members. It all starts with a simple, seemingly insignificant, decision by an individual to go to a small group meeting.

Many people get involved in small groups because they want friendships or fun. Most of the time they aren't disappointed. Others come along for loftier ideals—to study the Bible and get to know God better. But few people understand at the outset how important a small group can become in their life.

Jesus knew the power of working with a small group. The twelve men in His group were like you—young, enthusiastic and teachable. They came from different walks of life. They had different strengths and weaknesses, and they certainly all needed a radical transformation that only God could accomplish.

The Lord's unlikely small group went on to live lives fully devoted to Christ. They were known as those who turned the world upside down (Acts 17:6).

These disciples guarded what was entrusted to them, passing it on to others. Two thousand years later we are the beneficiaries.

You'll read many stories in this book of how God has worked through small groups. True, this is a book about leading small groups, but more importantly it's about our glorious God and His desire to change you and your world through small groups. Many have faithfully gone before you forging the way.

1.2

STORIES OF THOSE WHO'VE GONE BEFORE

In the fall of 1968, ten women at the University of Texas began meeting together. They were a mixed group of freshmen, sophomores, juniors and seniors. Half were in sororities. Most were committed to the Lord, although one of them, Marajen, was very young in her faith and barely involved in the Campus Crusade for Christ movement.

They didn't have a lot in common, but they came together to pray that God would change their lives and use them to change the world for Christ. How's that for a lofty purpose?

That year they studied 1 Corinthians and slowly opened their lives to each other and the Lord. The encouragement and support in the group helped everyone, especially Marajen, who was struggling in her Christian life.

Eventually each woman had a personal ministry on campus. Marajen was radically changed through the encouragement and prayers of the others. She began sharing Christ in the Theta house and over time saw twenty-nine of her sorority sisters trust Christ.

By the time all ten members of that original Bible study had graduated, God had answered their prayers in a big way. He had changed their lives and used them to make an impact in several sororities, plus a couple of dorms. Now it was time to influence the world beyond their campus.

Marajen decided to join the staff of Campus Crusade for Christ. Seven others also sensed God's call to go into full-time Christian work. One became a high school teacher and had a profound impact on students' lives. Another helped direct a major outreach in Atlanta.

Where are these ten women now? Nearly thirty years later, five of these women are still in full-time ministry. The others continue to walk with the Lord, ministering to their families and their communities. Over the years, thousands have come to know the Lord or been influenced because of their lives. Their small group started with the simple desire to grow in Christ and make a difference in the world. Only time will tell how many lives will be changed because of this small group.

In the fall of 1976, five men at the University of Alabama had a Bible study. Tuesday afternoons they met in a house near campus to study the Scriptures and talk about the small groups they were leading. The men had a lot of fun together—caravaning to Daytona Beach, FL, for a spring break evangelism conference, double dating, and playing hoops. The group lasted three years until graduation sent the men in different directions.

Today Ken and Scott are actively serving Christ in their businesses in Birmingham. Ken pioneered a ministry to young businessmen that later became a full-time ministry influencing thousands. Scott gives vital leadership to a

THE POWER OF A SMALL GROUP

"My brethren...let us plainly and freely tell one another what God has done for our souls. To this end you would do well, as others have done, to form yourselves into little companies of four or five each and meet once a week to tell each other what is in your hearts that you may pray for and comfort one another as need may require. None but they who have experienced it can tell the unspeakable advantage of such communion of souls. None, I think, that truly loves his own soul and his brethren as himself will be shy of opening his heart in order to have their advice, reproof, admonition and prayer as occasions require. A sincere person will esteem it one of the greatest blessings." — GEORGE WHITFIELD (Whitfield travelled extensively throughout America in the 18th century and was a major figure in the Great Awakening in America and the evangelical revival that swept Britain.)

growing and effective church. David and his wife have a home ministry to unwed mothers in Atlanta. They've led some of these mothers to Christ. The other two men both serve Christ full time with a missions group.

It's been nearly twenty years since the five of them met together amid their busy classes and activities at the University of Alabama. Each point to that small group as one of the highlights of their years at college. Their lives have never been the same, and their communities around them are different. It might have seemed like a casual decision back then to join a small group, but twenty years later the lasting effect of their experience begins to come to light.

Remember struggling Marajen from the group in 1968? Thirteen years later as a staff member with Campus Crusade, she spoke to a sorority at Texas Christian University where a sophomore named Judy sat in the audience listening intently. After hearing Marajen that evening, Judy decided to get involved in a Campus Crusade small group. She grew in her relationship with God and with the others in the group and developed a heart to influence women in the same way Marajen had influenced her. So she joined the staff of Campus Crusade.

JENNIFER'S CLOSE GROUP
I'm still in close contact with all the people in my first small group. We have gone through so much together, from dealing with school to the death and suicide of one woman's mom and dad. This taught me how important it is to be there for each other.

DAVID'S START
I went to my first small group meeting as a freshman. I learned that Christ was God, and I was blown away! Maybe I'd heard that before, but it never clicked. After that I really began to grow.

CHRISTINE'S BLOODY TALE
Being in nursing school was stressful, and I saw some gruesome things. Each week I looked forward to our small group where I could share what was going on. It was such a good outlet for me to talk about life and death and what really matters. (I'm sure some of the other members left half-sick.)

DIANA'S SNAPSHOT

At the beginning of my sophomore year, three friends and I began meet

ing together

to encourage one ano

ther and hold each another account

able in our walks with the

Lord. We really enjoyed each other, so we decided to room together the next fall. Over the next two years we had our own small group of sorts. We studied the Bible together, invited non-Christians into our apartment, and encouraged one another to honor the Lord with our lives. We even prayed that one day our husbands-to-be would actually like each other! More than twenty years have passed since we graduated, yet we are just as involved in each others' lives. We circulate a round robin letter every two months and carve out time to take a retreat together once or twice each year. Even though we live apart and have fifteen children between us that keep us busy, we are committed to each other. Who would have thought our small group in 1973 would result in such lifelong encouragers?

In 1988 while working at Vanderbilt University, Judy gathered a few sophomore women to be in a small group. They were in different sororities, came from different states; they all had different majors; and only two had met each other before. Some were new Christians, while two had been Christians for many years. This was a diverse group.

When it was time for the first meeting, Judy made brownies, popcorn and served diet Coke. Surely *that* would break the ice. To her amazement the women passed by the food completely—no one ate a thing. They didn't know each other. They didn't talk much. And they didn't even eat. Judy felt depressed. This group may never come together, she thought.

But Judy stuck with her commitment to build a group. At the next meeting, the women seemed more relaxed and conversation wasn't nearly as strained. They actually laughed together. At the end of their second meeting, Judy knew they had the potential to become unified.

As the weeks passed, the women showed they cared by getting involved in each others' lives and sharing in each others' walks with God. They became friends and spent time together outside of the group time. Judy watched in amazement as the women grew from shy, nervous acquaintances who wouldn't even eat brownies in front of each other to a close-knit group of friends who would scavenge her refrigerator at will!

At graduation the women signed up for their senior class trip to Panama City, FL. On the way out of town, they stopped by Judy's house with a card that said, "Something is Missing ..." Inside the card it said, "YOU." They kidnapped Judy and paid her expenses so she could be with them on their senior trip.

This group of women became more than just a casual group that studied the Bible. They continue to be friends and have served as each others bridesmaids. Their lives were changed, and they had significant ministries in others' lives—from women in their own sororities to those they ministered to on mission trips to Mexico and Russia.

Like the groups at the University of Texas and the University of Alabama, this group of women from Vanderbilt continues to influence others beyond the campus. One is a new mother, one works with children, one is a Christian counselor, one is a staff member with Campus Crusade, one is in medical school pursuing her dream of being a missionary doctor, and another is in business. Their careers are as different as their personalities and backgrounds, but all of them do what they do for the glory of God.

Time and space do not permit us to tell all the great small group stories that could be recounted here. Most groups start without a great splash or fanfare. None were led by perfect leaders with all the answers. But somehow, all across the country, in all different generations, God has worked in the midst of small groups. Only God knows the inside stories of the many lives which have been influenced in small groups.

Our prayer is that someday you'll add your small group story to those who have gone before you who have made a difference in this world. We pray we'll hear the story of how a great God worked through a faithful and available servant to graciously change lives. Now it's your turn.

Go ahead. Change the future.

FOR THOUGHT / DISCUSSION

1 Do you think God will do great things through your group? Why?

2 Share some of the ways you've been a beneficiary of those who have gone before you in their walks with the Lord. In what ways does this motivate you to pass God's Word on to others?

3 George Whitfield said that a "sincere person will esteem it (a small group) one of the greatest blessings." What reasons did he give? Do you agree or disagree?

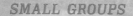

SMALL GROUPS
ACROSS
THE COUNTRY AND
WORLD HAVE HAD A TREMENDOUS
INFLUENCE IN PEOPLE'S LIVES. SOME INDIVIDUALS
HAVE COME TO KNOW CHRIST IN A SMALL GROUP,
OTHERS HAVE BEEN ENCOURAGED TO WALK
WITH GOD, MANY HAVE MADE
LIFELONG
FRIENDS.

SMALL GROUPS HAVE ALSO INFLUENCED
    THE ENVIRONMENT AROUND THEM, CHANGING FRATERNITY
HOUSES, APARTMENT COMPLEXES, RESIDENCE HALLS, AND
CAMPUSES. SIMPLY PUT, SMALL GROUPS ARE
    POWERFUL
        INSTRUMENTS

        GOD USES TO
                CHANGE
            LIVES.

2

DON'T TRAVEL ALONE!

2.1

THE POWER OF A SMALL GROUP

Alcoholics Anonymous, Overeaters Anonymous, and other support groups all understand the power of small groups to change behavior. Sales organizations utilize small groups to train for and encourage better sales. And, of course, Christians have met in small groups for two thousand years.

Why are small groups so powerful? For one thing, they help diverse individuals, usually only marginally connected, grow together as friends and work together toward similar spiritual goals.

These groups are effective because individuals draw strength and support from each other. Rarely does anyone benefit spiritually from being a lone ranger.

Small groups not only change the lives of those in the group, but they often bring about powerful change beyond the group. Families take notice as the son or daughter that left for college comes back with a growing relationship with God. Week after week friends and roommates watch this group get together at the end of the hall. They hear them laugh, watch them study the Bible, and see them reach out to each other as friends. It's appealing and they may want to be part of it.

Most small groups work together to give something back to their campus or community. They may put on an evangelistic event in their dorm or greek house, feed the homeless, or help out with another need on campus. Never underestimate the power of God working through a group to change lives!

HOLLY'S SURPRISE

I was a sophomore who really wanted to study the Bible but didn't see any need for being in a group. I figured the Christian life was me, God and the Bible. In my mind, the small talk which often characterized small groups was just a waste of time. But I decided to give it a shot. Much to my amazement, I really enjoyed it. I needed the insights of others and their friendship. I benefited both in my personal life and in my walk with the Lord. Today, the women I got to know in that small group are some of my closest friends.

14

2.2

CRUCIAL ELEMENTS

Though groups may include a variety of members, personalities and people from a wide range of backgrounds, there are some elements which characterize every effective Christian small group. A prospering small group will have each of these elements: Christ-centered focus, community, each person richly experiencing Christ, progressive life-change and outward impact. Each area will be developed throughout this book.

1 Quality Biblical Content

This might come as a surprise, but small group Bible studies study the Bible. Central to the Christian faith is the belief that God has revealed Himself to us in His Word. But the ultimate goal of studying the Bible together is to point the group to Christ, not to view Bible knowledge as an end in itself, but to see the

Bible as a map that leads us to Christ.

Your group needs to experience Christ, not just learn more about the Bible, as valuable as that is. In no way do we want to move away from the Bible—it is the Word of God— but as you study the Scripture you want to help your group to see the person to whom the Scriptures point, that is Jesus. This is not to look to find Jesus in every text but to look to discover how the text relates and points to Christ and his redemptive work.

"And beginning with Moses and all the Prophets, he interpreted to them in all the Scriptures the things concerning himself....They said to each other, 'Did not our hearts burn within us while he talked to us on the road, while he opened to us the Scriptures.'"
— LUKE 24:27, 32

"If you believed Moses, you would believe me; for he wrote of me."
—ISAIAH 40:8

"The grass withers and the flowers fall, but the word of our God stands forever." —ISAIAH 40:8

15

"All Scripture is God-breathed and is useful for teaching, rebuking, correcting and training in righteousness." —II TIMOTHY 3:16

BOB'S NAPKIN
The greatest thing I learned from Bob, my Bible study leader, was the importance of God's Word. We were studying Romans and he challenged us to read it fifty times by the end of the semester. We laughed at him, but the more we read it, the more we learned. One day at McDonald's he took out a napkin and drew sixteen empty squares on it, one for each chapter. He told me to fill in the squares, telling him about every chapter in Romans. To my amazement I could do it. Bob's leadership, and that group, made God's Word come alive for me.

2 Community

Community is the sense within the group that members are a team, bonded together as friends and committed to each other's well-being and growth.

MISSY'S FRIEND

Tonya knew that as she and Bill got more and more serious in their dating relationship they would run into some intense temptation. They both decided to honor God in their physical relationship and part of doing that was having someone to whom they were accountable. Tonya asked me to be that person. Every week when we got together to talk, she knew I would ask if she and Bill had kept their hands off each other. It's not that I was responsible for their success, but I could remind her of the decision she and Bill had made to remain pure. And I could pray for her and Bill. We all got to attend their wedding—it was a great day!

GREG'S GROUP

I remember the awkward tension in that first group. Some guys looked like they were dying just being in the room. Looking back on it, I would have paid five bucks for someone to crack a joke and break the mood. That all changed over time as the guys got to know each other. Two months later the guys were up half the night planning a creative date with a women's group. I couldn't believe they were the same bunch of guys.

16

This doesn't happen all at once, but healthy, growing groups have an increasing sense of community. Over time, individuals rejoice together, and share in sorrow together. These groups move from being "Tom's group" to "our group," as members begin to take ownership of the group. The leader can help facilitate this, but community is not primarily a leadership issue. Rather, it's a oneness that becomes apparent when individuals come to value others in the group. Chapter 6 will give you insight into understanding community and some ideas on how to nurture this in your group.

3 Each Person Richly Experiencing Christ

As a leader your role is to stimulate group members to encounter and experience Christ for themselves. One of the most intimidating things that a small group leader faces is thinking that they have to have all the answers—the "map" memorized. Leaders don't need to have all the answers, but they do need to be experiencing Christ for themselves and know how to point others to Him. This comes from knowing people's greatest needs (chapters 4 and 5) having an understanding of how real change happens (chapter 5) and being skilled at asking good questions that engage the heart (chapter 8).

You want each person in your group to taste, see, and personally encounter Christ as you come to the Scriptures.

4 Progressive Life-Change

Successful small groups are about life-change. On the roadtrip of life, we all hit potholes, dead ends, construction zones, and pileups—sometimes twenty cars or more. As a result of the wear-and-tear brought on by life's challenges, each week the members of your group show up in less than showroom condition, sometimes in need of some serious bodywork. Their condition may be obvious, or not so obvious.

As a leader (in need of your own bodywork, of course) you want to allow the Scriptures to expose our brokenness, our potholes, and then follow the passage as it points toward a solution and ultimately to a person, Jesus Christ. This is how life-change happens. If a group stops short of being a catalyst for life-change, it has fallen short of all God intends for the group.

5 Outward Impact

A small group needs an outlet to put into action what they are learning. As the group reaches out to others, at least two things happen: the group is strengthened and more lives are changed. Seeking to make an impact is a difficult step for many groups because it's safer to become ingrown. But virtually all groups need to take the key step of turning the focus of the group from "getting" to "giving." We'll talk more about this in Chapter 10.

17

TODD'S LINE
When leading a small group, nothing beats the feeling when someone says, "I wouldn't be where I am today without you."

RICK'S INFLUENCE
One day I asked the men in my group, "Who has been the most influential person in your life, apart from your parents?" One of the guys looked straight at me and said, "You've had the greatest impact on my life."

KIRSTEN'S DATES
The seven of us decided to have a fun night so we asked seven guys along. We called it "Rotate-a-Date." We planned seven different activities for the night—dinner, ping pong, singing with a guitar overlooking the city, etc. For each activity we had a different date. Maybe it's a record worthy of Guiness...seven dates in one night!

2.3

WHAT TO EXPECT

Of course, there is no way to predict the outcome of your small group. Students in your group might sit at your feet and hang on your every word, or they may hide in the closet when they hear you come to the door to remind them about the Bible study. They may laugh at your jokes and eat your brownies, or they may listen politely and leave quickly. You just never know what will happen. You can, however, expect at least four things to take place.

1 *Expect it to take time for your group to grow in maturity and commitment.*
There are no shortcuts to maturity. You'll probably feel frustrated by the sporadic attendance in your group, which is often true of new groups. Group members' commitment will develop as they grow in their relationships with the Lord and get to know you and each other. It takes time.

2 *Expect to face challenging situations.*

Naive Statements from New Group Leaders
"Surely everyone will come back each week."
...Yeah, unless they have a date, homework, laundry, need a nap, "forgot," etc...
"Everyone will be best friends from the start." ...Not likely when they're still using name tags and all.
"Leading a group will take about a half hour a week."
...Yeah, right.
"Everyone in the group will think I'm brilliant."
...Guess again, Einstein.

Leading a small group is always a challenge. Things will happen in group that you won't expect. For instance, what if no one shows up, or perhaps a group member's personal crisis diverts you from ever getting to the lesson. Sometimes individuals in the group will be a challenge to you. When you step out in faith to be involved in the lives of your group members, you never know what you'll encounter. Trust God to work on your behalf. We've addressed some typical challenges in Chapter 9.

Influencing your small group takes spending time with them. However, no matter how challenging your group gets, God will use you as you seek Him and step out in faith. Paul reminded the Corinthians, "Al-

18

What do you expect from leading your small group? Some small group leaders are fearful their small group will never go anywhere. Other leaders are sure their group is destined for glory. Both views are incorrect to some degree at least. God reminds us in Psalm 127:1, "Unless the Lord builds the house, its builders labor in vain." Your small group will only be powerful if God builds it. Be honest about your expectations, but place them under God's control and abide in Him as you lead.

ways give yourselves fully to the work of the Lord, because you know that your labor in the Lord is not in vain" (1 Corinthians 15:58).

3 Expect gratifying results.

Most group leaders find the experience of leading a small group tremendously rewarding. You may have the joy of seeing people come to Christ or begin to walk with the Lord. The apostle John wrote, "I have no greater joy than to hear that my children are walking in the truth" (3 John 4).

Not only will you likely find leading a group profitable for God's kingdom and beneficial to you personally, but it can be a lot of fun as well.

4 Expect to grow in your relationship with God.

Sometimes the group leader will learn more from leading than the individuals in the group. By stepping out in faith, you can expect God to change your life as you minister to others because you'll understand Scripture better, and you'll see how biblical truth is worked out in a person's life, including your own.

CONCLUSION

So, why travel in a small group? God has created us with a need for each other. We need each other for encouragement, and, hey, it's much more fun than being alone. Even Barbara Streisand knows that people who need people are the luckiest people in the world. What? You don't know that song? Ask your parents.

God never intended us to live the Christian life alone. Each of us are a unique part of the body of Christ. God created us to use our strengths and abilities to build each other up. In small groups, different members of the body of Christ work together to encourage each other and build up the entire body of Christ. There's something unique about how God works in and through a group.

FOR THOUGHT / DISCUSSION

1 What do you expect from leading a small group? Be honest. How will these expectations influence how you lead the group?

2 Christian small groups share much in common with many secular small groups. What makes Christian small groups distinctively different?

3 Look at the five elements of a good small group. Think about the groups you've been involved in. Which of these five elements were present? Which were most meaningful to you? Why?

4 The believers in Berea (Acts 17:10–12) would be great people to have in your small group. What can you do as a leader to help encourage this kind of attitude toward the Scriptures?

21

LEADING A GROUP FOR THE FIRST TIME CAN BE INTIMIDATING, AN[D]

NOT ALONE. "WHAT IF SOMEONE ASKS ME A QUESTION I CAN'T ANSWER?"

"WHAT IF THE GROUP CLAMS UP... OR GOES FROM

3

IF YOU'RE WONDERING ABOUT YOUR QUALIFICATIONS TO LEAD, YOU'RE NOT ALONE. ALL LEADERS DOUBT THEMSELVES FROM TIME TO TIME. "WHAT IF SOMEONE KNOWS MORE THAN I DO?" THEY MIGHT. "WHAT IF THE CONVERSATION GOES FROM TANGENT TO TANGENT...OR FALLS APART COMPLETELY?" IT HAPPENS SOMETIMES.

CHAPTER 3

PASSING THE DRIVER'S TEST

3.1

FOUR ESSENTIAL QUALITIES

Leading a group can be frightening if you focus on the millions of things that could go wrong. Don't worry. God takes pleasure in using people who don't have all the answers, but who are in the process of learning. The Bible is full of stories of how God used imperfect people to accomplish His great purpose.

What, then, does it take? Perfection is not required. If it were, none of us could lead a small group. But all small group leaders need to be in the process of developing certain qualities: godly character, compassion, competence, and commitment.

1 Authentically Experiencing Christ

The character of a group leader is crucial. It's inevitable that members in your group will look to you as a spiritual role model. You know you're not perfect, so take off the pressure and don't even pretend to be perfect. Be real and model an eager desire to grow in your own walk with the Lord. You have the same needs as those in your group: the need to be in God's Word, the need to confess your sins, and the need to daily seek to honor God with your life.

"Don't let anyone look down on you because you are young, but set an example for the believers in speech, in life, in love, in faith and in purity." — 1 TIMOTHY 4:12

"Be diligent in these matters; give yourself wholly to them, so that everyone may see your progress." — 1 TIMOTHY 4:15

Personal progress is the key. No one would ever lead a group if they waited until their character is perfectly godly. On the other hand, if a leader is living in disobedience to the Lord, it will be difficult for those in the group to learn to walk with the Lord.

Jesus taught, "A student is not above his teacher, but everyone who is fully trained will be like his teacher" (Luke 6:40). Jesus did not say, "Everyone, when he is fully trained, will be like his teaching." It's sobering, but true, your life will have great influence on the people in your group. They are watching you to see your personal commitment to walk with the Lord.

BEN'S PUSH-UPS

Our group memorized scripture each week. Each time we got together we had to recite our verse and we had to do a push-up for every word missed. Some weeks a lot of push-ups were done by the guys. One week our group leader, Dave, had us recite our verses, and as usual we made many mistakes. But he said this week we didn't have to do any push-ups. Instead Dave did a push-up for each of our mistakes. He wanted us to understand that Christ had done that for us. I've never forgotten that lesson or Dave's example.

2 Compassion

Compassion is emotion turned into action. Sympathy causes us to feel for others, compassion causes us to do something about it. As Jesus viewed the large crowds, He "had compassion on them, because they were harassed and helpless, like sheep without a shepherd" (Matthew 9:36). Jesus willingly gave His life for the lost, harassed and helpless—following through on His compassion.

As a small group leader you need compassion for others. You need to truly care about people and be actively involved in giving to them. It's been

CHANIN'S CARE

I once discipled a girl named Aimee. Only a few weeks before we met, Aimee had lost her parents and her brother-in-law. As if that weren't enough, in the fall she found out her sister had lymphoma cancer. While at the Dallas Christmas Conference, Aimee learned her sister died. All I could do was hold her and cry with her. It really taught me that leading a small group often involves being intimately involved in the lives of individuals.

KIRK'S TIMING

I can't tell you how many times something would come up in my group that God had dealt with me literally the day before. It was funny that God knew ahead of time what I needed to lead my group, and He prepared me for it. I was never more than a step ahead of the people in my group.

said, "People don't care what you know until they know that you care." It's true. Your love and concern speaks as loudly as anything you teach them. Giving and caring for people in your group is one of the greatest privileges and responsibilities of leadership. It's a key to the success of any group.

What happens when people say they'll be there but don't show? Or when something promised doesn't happen? As the leader your first response might be hurt or anger. Compassion allows you to look past your fear of failing and to the needs and concerns of those group members. It enables you to think: What pressures might they be facing? How can I encourage them? How can I let them know they really are wanted as part of the group? A compassionate leader is focused on the needs of the group members.

3 Competence

Moses is an example of someone who lacked competence (or at least thought he did). God thought differently. He said to Moses, "I want you to lead the Israelites out of Egypt." Moses retorted, "No way. There's no way I can lead the Israelites. They won't believe me. I might say something stupid. Who am I that I should ask Pharaoh to let the Israelites leave Egypt? Can't you send someone else, like maybe Aaron? Yeah, Aaron would be perfect. Great hair. White teeth. Winning smile. You know he's a communication major, don't you?"

But God didn't want someone else. He didn't want Aaron. He wanted Moses. God simply assured him, "I will be with you. That's enough for you" (Exodus 3–4). Over and over God uses seemingly inadequate people by making them adequate. Gideon noted, "My clan is the weakest in Manasseh, and I am the least in my family" (Judges 6:15), and Paul said, "I did not come… with eloquence or superior wisdom" (1 Corinthians 2:1).

Competence involves two issues. First, as you depend upon the Lord to use you, He makes you adequate. Paul sets forth faithfulness, not giftedness, as the prerequisite for those who are to teach others in 2 Timothy 2:2. God is looking for men and women who fear Him and walk humbly before Him. These are "competent" group leaders. Second, you are also responsible to develop leadership skills. These skills will develop over time, and reading this book is a great place to start, but nothing takes the place of actually learning as you go.

28

MAURICE'S WAKE-UP

My first group at Ohio State was a disaster. I had to literally wake up each of the three men in the middle of the afternoon to drag them to Bible study. I couldn't figure out why they weren't more committed. Then my group leader attended the Bible study and pointed out that I lectured the entire time, while everyone else dozed. I learned that day I needed to develop competence by developing skills in leading a group discussion.

JIMMY & NATHAN'S PERSISTENCE

We never realized leading would be so hard. After one semester of leading a small group at the University of North Texas, we found out it was hard getting the guys to show up, and even if they did show, they weren't always into it. Our leader always reminded us that the group we co-led wasn't a failure. By the end of the semester, twelve guys were regularly involved. However, leading the group meant hours of phone calls, dropping by dorm rooms, inviting guys over for pizza and Monday Night Football, or for Friday night videos when no one had dates.

How to Be a Leader No One Wants to Follow
- *Put on a religious facade for your group, but live differently outside of group.*
- *Be more concerned about whether people show up for your group than how they are doing in life.*
- *Subtly let the group know you've gone beyond them in the Christian life. You are the leader. You used to have their struggles.*
- *Tell the group you can't make it next week because you're too busy.*
- *Assume you're a natural born group leader and don't need to work at leading the group. You've done quite well winging other things, so try it in your group.*
- *Be more concerned with how well you're leading, not how much the group is learning.*
- *Be sure to tell your group how much you know.*

4 Commitment

Leading a group takes time, emotional energy and effort. Just like anything else worth doing, there is a cost involved. Students who play varsity sports, write for the school newspaper, or lead a fraternity or sorority, all pay a price for something they desire to accomplish. Small group leaders do the same, but it is worth it to see God transform lives.

Sometimes your small group will flourish, and you'll think this is the greatest thing you've ever done. At other times you might wonder how you ever got to be captain of this sinking ship. Commitment will keep you trusting the Lord and sticking it out. Just think, at one point even Paul wrote, "Demas, because he has loved this world, has deserted me and has gone to Thessalonica. Crescens has gone to Galatia, and Titus to Dalmatia. Only Luke is with me" (2 Timothy 4:10,11). Everybody left Paul but Luke. Paul knew what it was like to stick it out!

Sometimes individuals in your group might disappoint you, hurt your feelings, or totally blow you off. It's tough being involved with people because they are fickle and sinful (as you are sometimes). But they're worth it.

You may find it helpful to look up some biblical references for each of these four areas and pray that God would further deepen and develop them in your life.

Authentically Experiencing Christ

Colossians 3:1–17, Matthew 22:34–40,
Ephesians 4:17–5:21

Compassion

Matthew 9:35–38, 1 Thessalonians 2:1–12

Competency

2 Corinthians 3:4–6, Exodus 3:1–4:17

Commitment

Colossians 1:28–29, 1 Corinthians 15:58,
Acts 20:17–38

30

CONCLUSION

The prerequisites to leading a small group—godly character, compassion, competence, commitment—are areas which can progressively develop in each of us over time. God doesn't measure your success by how many students you recruit to go to conferences or by how many stick with your groups. Your success as a group leader is ultimately measured by Jesus Christ. He simply wants you to use your unique gifts and abilities to step out in faith and teach others about Him.

People are God's ultimate concern. When Jesus returns, He will not come back for libraries, cars or the Grand Canyon. He will come back for people. When God became man, He said His purpose was to "seek and save that which was lost" (Luke 19:10). He was talking about people. His heart for people is so contagious that those who follow Him become "fishers of men" (Matthew 4:19). As a small group leader, you have the great privilege of being involved with that which is dearest to God—people.

FOR THOUGHT / DISCUSSION

1 Which of these four qualities—godly character, compassion, competency, commitment—seems most overwhelming to you? Why? Which quality seems to be most natural for you?

2 Talk about a group you've been in previously. Discuss how the character of the leader influenced the group.

3 Do you think it is more important for a group leader to be compassionate or competent? Why?

4 In 1 Peter 5:2–4, Peter gives instructions to the elders about leading those under their care. What qualities do you see in Peter's "small group leaders"? How can you demonstrate these qualities in your specific situation?

31

Maybe you're looking at the qualifications for leadership and you're thinking, There's no way I stack up to those standards. I can barely carve out enough time in my schedule for a quiet time. Remember that none of us, by ourselves, are adequate to be used by God to change lives. If you trust Him by stepping out in faith to give of yourself to others, He will use you.

"Such confidence as this is ours through Christ before God. Not that we are competent in ourselves to claim anything for ourselves, but our competence comes from God. He has made us competent as ministers of a new covenant..."
—11 Corinthians 3:4–6

Dear Jessica,

   I couldn't believe it. You're gonna die when you hear this. I was going to visit my dad in Seattle over Christmas and got on the wrong plane. I checked the screen at the airport for departures at least twice and thought for sure the sign at the gate said, 'Departure to Seattle.'

   Well, I'm sitting there on the plane with my headphones on, listening to a new CD I just got. Of course I ignored those safety instructions and fell asleep. Rick and I had gone out to a midnight movie the night before.

   About halfway through the trip, I wake up to an announcement over the speakers. The captain told us we were flying over Lake Ontario and that we'd be in Boston

in less than an hour. BOSTON!? Man, I freaked.

I ran up to the flight attendant and asked her where we were going. Again, 'We'll be in Boston in about an hour.' I told her what my deal was. She couldn't believe it. She looked at my ticket and saw I wasn't lying.

I found out in Boston later that the gates back in Indianapolis for Boston and Seattle were right next to each other. The airline paid for my flight to Seattle since they made the mistake of letting me on the plane. My dad would have killed me if he had to pay for another flight.

I'll see you back at school in a few weeks. Have a great Christmas.

Love, Amanda

SO, WHERE YA' HEADED?

People like Amanda take wrong turns all the time, but most people don't start out on a trip without having a destination in mind. Good road trips take planning. You need to know your destination, why you want to get there, and the best route to take you there. If you don't plan, there is little likelihood that you'll make it.

Leading a small group also takes planning. Before you begin your group ask yourself these questions: Why am I leading this group? Where do I want it to go? How do I plan to get there? Your answers will dictate many things, including the content, the length, and how you run your group time. Before you can answer these questions however, you must know something about the people in your group.

4.1

ASSESSING THEIR NEEDS

It's critical to get to know the needs of those in your group. If you offer content that misses the needs of your group, they'll have little desire to return. For example, if most in your group aren't sure they are Christians, it's doubtful they'll enjoy a group lesson on reaching the world for Christ. They probably won't come back.

You may have heard of "felt needs" and "real needs." For example, people have the felt need to be loved and accepted. But people also have the real need of an intimate relationship with God and forgiveness. When the real need goes unmet, the felt need takes priority.

To clarify, I want to change the titles of "felt needs" and "real needs" to "surface needs" and "heart-level needs." Surface needs are usually obvious. It's when a girl in your Bible study admits that she has been sleeping with her boyfriend. It's when a guy is struggling with pornography. It's when the newer believer keeps getting drunk at the bars with his friends. But below the surface needs are heart-level needs that, if left untouched, will continue to manifest themselves in surface needs.

But what if you have Sally Sanctification or Bible Bob in your group and they have no obvious surface needs? The thing to remember is that Sally and Bob have the very same heart-level needs as those with more obvious surface needs. In fact, just like the girl who uses her boyfriend for love and acceptance, Sally may be using religious pretense to win acceptance from the religious community. Bible Bob may be addicted to the high of looking more religious than others just like the guy who's addicted to beer. In fact, Sally Sanctification may be using *her* boyfriend, not for love gained through sex, but for a sense of security. If he left, would her world come crashing down?

Your goal as a leader is to move below the surface and uncover the heart-level needs that drive all of us. In other words, we all share a fallen/broken heart condition that needs the healing of Christ applied.

We'll talk more about heart-level needs and how Christ meets those needs in the next chapter. For now, let's practically look at how to assess the surface needs of your group.

Pray

Pray for insight and wisdom. Ask God for sensitivity to the needs of your group.

Observe

Begin by observing as much as you can about your group members. You can learn plenty from just watching their actions.

- Are they comfortable talking about being a Christian?

- What do you observe about their relationships with Christians and non-Christians? Their roommates?

- How do they interact with others? Are they shy? Outgoing? Overbearing? Controlling?

- Are they involved in church? A Christian group?

- What can you observe about their walk with the Lord?

- Do they seem hesitant to be involved in a small group? If so, why?

- What kind of Bible do they bring? Does it look like it's ever been used?

37

JILL'S BOMB

When Melinda, Lee Anne, and I went to our first small group at Texas A&M, we were pretty excited about the idea of being in a Bible study together. The leader, Jill, lost ground quickly by announcing, "You probably already know this, but let's go through it anyway." We weren't exactly won over. The "discussion" didn't help either. Jill tried to field test her elementary education skills by asking questions such as, "OK now, what did Jesus do in this verse? He died for our sins. Good. Let's go to the next question." Soon an uneasy silence fell over the room.

As we laughed and talked on the way home, we made a unanimous decision— no one wanted to go where this group was headed. Next Thursday, no one wanted to go, but we felt sorry for Jill. We figured someone should show, so we drew straws to see who would make the token appearance. For the next few weeks we followed the same routine, drawing straws to pick the "winner."

Ask

Although you may learn a good deal from observing those in your group, your best source of information about their needs will come from asking them. This is especially true when you begin to lead a group. Your observations aren't always as helpful and accurate as what you can learn directly from group members. When you are with group members, ask a few informal questions. For example:

- Why do you have an interest in being in a Bible study?

- Have you ever been involved in a church before? What was it like?

- What is your spiritual background?

- What would you like to get out of this Bible study?

These questions will help you get to know the spiritual needs of your group.

Survey

There are two ways to do surveys. The easiest is to hand out 3x5 cards in the group and get their input. A second type of survey is longer but will give you more information. They would answer it outside of group time and give it to you later.

THE 3x5 SURVEY: Choose questions that are appropriate for your group and indicate that you will use their answers to help in your planning. Hand out 3x5 cards and let them jot down their input. Some questions you might ask:

- If asked to describe my relationship with the Lord at the present, I would use these adjectives:

- When I struggle in my relationship with the Lord it is generally in these areas:

- If I could have one question answered about how to live the Christian life, it would be...

GARY'S WAKE-UP CALL
One of the men who continued on in my Bible study later faded from the movement after my group ended. I found out why the next semester. I read his article in the school's newspaper where he wrote about his coming-out as a confident and proud homosexual. Talk about a wake-up call! I felt like after all those months I didn't even know the guy.

• The one thing I would like to get out of this group is...

THE LONGER SURVEY: You can gather more information by giving a longer survey to group members and asking them to fill it out. It would probably be best to do this outside of group time. Introduce the survey by saying you want the group to best meet their needs, so you'd like their input. The sample survey in the appendix will give you some ideas. Don't assume you know the struggles and questions of group members.

> ### DAVE'S HOG LOINS
> *I was leading a group of agriculture majors at the University of Nebraska and stepped into an interesting conversation they were having about hog judging—how to know which hog had the best loin. Being from Detroit, I had a hard time, at first, relating to these guys. I realized before I would ever begin to understand them and what they needed, I had to get to know their world. They taught me about hogs, and I taught them about city life.*

As you're thinking through the needs of your group, ask a veteran group leader or a Campus Crusade staff member for input. Since the ability to understand and meet the needs of people grows with experience, their input will be helpful.

Cultural Trends for College Students

Several studies reveal various trends in our culture that might be helpful as you get to know your group. Since you are probably in the same generation as those in your group (unless you've been in school a long time), you're probably safe in assuming that students are like you. Here are some noteworthy trends of students.

• *At least 50 percent of the students are coming from broken homes. Divorce is often viewed as an inevitable part of the marriage process. In the not too distant future, most Americans will believe that a life spent with the same partner is both unusual and unnecessary. So, a group might have needs to learn about God's love and faithfulness, forgiveness, or marriage.*

- *Most students are highly influenced by the media. Above all else, college students love to be entertained. This passion for high-gloss, big-screen entertainment is confirmed by the movie studios, who unabashedly admit that they develop most of their movies with the college audience in mind. People under the age of 25 account for more than half of the revenues generated by movie theaters today. And they are responsible for several billion dollars more in revenues generated by the sale and rental of movies and video games. So, perhaps you could use media in your small group, such as looking at the intro to an MTV clip or part of a TV show.*

- *Most students are skeptical of absolutes. "There is one thing a professor can be absolutely certain of: almost every student entering the university believes, or says he believes, that truth is relative" (Allan Bloom, The Closing of the American Mind). Maybe your group needs to learn about the character of God and the authority of His Word.*

- *Many students are sexually experienced and may presently be sexually active. "And among [college students], more than three-quarters claim that they have engaged in sexual intercourse with other single adults. Today, only 23 percent of the single [college students] profess to being virgins" (Barna, Invisible Generation, p145). It's probably safe to assume most groups need to address the issues of sex, sexual immorality, purity and forgiveness.*

40

- *Because Eastern religions (such as Hinduism and Buddhism), New Age and cults are gaining influence, students may combine various elements from different faiths. George Barna notes, "It is likely that from Christianity they will borrow Jesus' philosophy of love and acceptance. From Eastern religions they will borrow ideas related to each person being his or her own god, the center of the universe, capable of creating and resolving issues through his or her own power and intelligence" (Barna, The Frog in the Kettle, p141). So, maybe your group needs to examine the uniqueness of Jesus or the deity of Christ.*

How to Kill Your Group
- *Don't make an effort to find out the needs of your group. Trust your feelings.*
- *Choose content that seems most fun to you, like whale hunting. Never mind they all happen to be members of Greenpeace.*
- *Just assume whatever you do in the Bible will be just fine for your group...like studying the book of Revelation.*
- *Write up a purpose statement, forget what it says, and never refer to it again.*
- *Don't worry about how many weeks you run your group. You'll be able to tell when it has run long enough by the empty spaces on the couch.*

4.2

DETERMINING YOUR DESTINATION

Once you get a grip on the needs of your group members, it's time to work on the purpose for your group. How, specifically, can God use you to help meet the needs of those in your group? What content will be most helpful? How many weeks should the group run? These decisions are best prayerfully made with a veteran group leader if possible. Their experience will help you choose content and structure your group.

Here are some questions to help you think through determining the purpose and objectives of your group:

1 *How does your small group fit into the big picture of the ongoing ministry on your campus?*
Your small group leader or staff member can help you think through your small group's purpose in light of that overall strategy.

- Is your small group trying to develop future leaders?

- Is your small group part of a plan to reach a section of campus?

- Is your focus on evangelism? Building new believers? Training believers to minister to others?

2 *What are the specific needs of your group?*
- Do group members understand and apply the basics of the Christian life (assurance of salvation, dealing with sin, etc.)?

- Do group members take the initiative to study God's Word and grow in Christ or are they dependent on someone else to motivate them spiritually?

- Which character and conduct issues need attention (gossip, moral standards, thought life, integrity, etc.)?

- What are their daily concerns and struggles (studying, finances, relationships, family concerns, etc.)?

41

- Do group members have a growing concern for those who don't know Christ? Do they know how to share the gospel with non-Christians?

3 *What do you want to be true of your group members when the group ends?*

- What growth would you like to see in their lives? What would tell you they are growing in their relationship with the Lord? How can you help them develop consistent, personal time in God's Word and in prayer?

- How would you like to see your group members change so as to live holy and godly lives?

- What steps would you like to see them take to reach out to others? Or pray for someone? Maybe they need to prepare their testimony, invite someone to a weekly meeting, or learn how to share their faith.

- How will their lives be different if they consistently surrender areas of their lives to Christ (studies, finances, relationships, family, etc.)?

42

MEETING THE NEEDS OF COLLEGE FRESHMEN

If your group has freshmen, you can be relatively certain these are important issues for them...

- *Advice on professors, classes, majors, study skills, scheduling time, etc.*

- *Input on how the campus works (administration, etc)*

- *Help making friends at school.*

- *Advice on finding a church.*

- *Help getting around town and campus.*

After you've considered the needs of those in your group, take time to write out the needs of your group and a preliminary purpose statement. You can always adjust it later as you get to know your group better.

You may be thinking, This is such a hassle. I just wanted to lead a small group. However, the more you know about the strengths and struggles of those in your group, the better you'll be able to point them to God's solutions. As they see God's Word change their lives they'll be more likely to come back. Seeing God change lives is the point, isn't it?

Many group leaders get discouraged when people just don't show up. Often this is caused by offering solutions to problems no one seems to have. Take time to plan for your group. Give them biblical solutions that make a difference—give them something they are hungry for. Brownies help, but that's another chapter.

4.3

CHOOSING YOUR CONTENT

Like any trip you take, not only do you need to know where you're going, but also how to get there. Once you've determined your destination (the purpose of your group) you're ready to choose your route, the content of your small group. You'll also need to determine how long the group should meet to accomplish your purpose.

There are many potential topics which you could study that would be beneficial to your group. As you review the purpose of your group and assessment of their needs, consider the following:

1 Have your group members been in a Bible study before? What did they study?

2 What principles, or topics, would benefit them most at this stage in their Christian walk?

3 What are their crucial needs? Sometimes students want to study a difficult book of the Bible such as Revelation or the latest hot Christian book. Although this may be a felt need for them, their real need is to understand and apply the basic truths of the Christian life such as salvation, forgiveness, the Spirit-filled life, and how to learn and apply God's Word.

4 How many weeks should this group meet? Take into account their commit-

43

ment level, how well they know each other, and the time constraints of school. Choose a length that complements your purpose. For some groups, such as evangelistic Bible studies, a shorter time period is better.

After you've determined your purpose and gathered all the information you can about your group members, make a decision about what content and time frame will be best for your purpose. Ask the Lord for wisdom and pray about different options. You most likely won't receive your answer on a piece of paper descending from heaven, but it makes great sense to seek God's wisdom. Interact with your Campus Crusade staff member or your group leader. You'll find their input valuable.

Case Study: Geoff
Geoff is starting a small group. He needs to determine the purpose for his group and, in light of this purpose, the best content and duration of the group.

"I have seven freshmen from my dorm in my group. They all say they are Christians, but I don't think they see how God relates to their daily lives. A few recently placed their trust in Christ. They all need help in understanding the Spirit-filled life. When I took an informal survey to see what they wanted from the group, many of the men seemed to have needs and questions in the areas of dating, sex and stress. I've also noticed that many of them hang out with guys who party a lot."

"I talked to Greg, the staff guy who's my leader, about what content I should cover in my group. He explained how my group fit into the overall purpose of our campus ministry. After talking it over, and asking God for wisdom, we decided upon this purpose statement for my group: 'The purpose of my group is to help establish these freshmen guys in the basics of walking with God and start giving them a vision for reaching out to others.'"

"It seemed like the best time frame for a study with this purpose was about a semester. This gives the guys time to get to know each other and to begin to apply truths they are learning in group. Greg helped me choose the content to best achieve this purpose in light of the guys in my group. We chose some basic topics related to their walk with the Lord and others that are relevant issues they raised that effect their walk with the Lord."

Geoff's Purpose and Content Worksheet
1 *After prayerfully assessing the needs of my group members, I think their basic spiritual needs are:*
Assurance of salvation; What to do when I sin; How to be filled with the Holy

Spirit; How to let God direct and empower me daily; Spending time with God; Sharing God's love with others

2 I think their basic felt needs are:
Dating; Sexual purity; Drinking; Stress; Better grades

3 In light of their needs and the overall purpose of our campus ministry, the purpose of my group will be:
To help establish these freshmen guys in the basics of walking with God and to start giving them a vision for reaching out to others.

4 This purpose is best accomplished by meeting this many weeks: one semester

5 I think that the best topics to fulfill the purpose of our group are:

6 I will pray God changes the lives of those in my group in these ways:

Try filling out questions 5 & 6 for your own group.

45

CONCLUSION

Assessing the needs of your group, determining the purpose of your group, and choosing the content for the group: we've covered a lot in this chapter! Many group leaders fail to think through these issues. They think, "Oh, we'll just study the Bible." Well, that beats studying Freud or Marx, but it doesn't necessarily help your group members relate God's Word to their present struggles.

An unplanned Bible study causes more stress on the leader and less learning for the group members. A leader can generate a great discussion on a topic but that doesn't mean it is the most helpful for people. Take time to plan; it will help you maintain an effective, life-changing small group.

FOR THOUGHT / DISCUSSION

1 Share experiences in your life when you were supposed to learn something, but what was being taught had no interest to you. (For example, high school history? a small group lesson? a sermon?) How did your lack of motivation affect your learning? Share experiences when something was taught that really connected with a need in your life. How did your intrinsic motivation affect your learning?

2 *What are some ways you can foster goal ownership in your group?*

3 *What are the risks of choosing topcis that interest you instead of topics that interest the group? What are the benefits of choosing topics which you are learning at the time?*

4 *Talk about Geoff's case study and work through the Purpose / Content sheet for this group. The group consists of sophomore women who are at different maturity levels in their Christian lives. Their key interests are the opposite sex, grades and security. Most are from divorced homes. They seem to have little knowledge of the Bible, and want to have successful careers and relationships more than they want to know God. They seem like they are willing to come to the group and have some interest in studying the Bible.*

EMPTY

TANK

?

"What if I'm still totally clueless about my group members' needs? Is it possible I could teach the wrong material?" These are good questions, but don't worry. If you faithfully teach and apply God's Word, your group members will benefit. As your group opens up, you'll get to know their needs better and, if necessary, you can adjust your content. Spend time with your group members and ask for their honest feedback. They'll tell you if you're addressing areas which are helping them.

47

WHEN YOU ARE ON A ROAD TRIP IT'S USUALLY THE ROAD THAT'S UNDER CONSTRUCTION, NOT THE TRAVELER. BUT IN A SMALL GROUP IT'S THE TRAVELERS WHO ARE IN THE PROCESS OF BEING CHANGED. LIFE-CHANGE IS A CRUCIAL PRODUCT OF SMALL GROUPS. IF THE DISCUSSION IN YOUR GROUP GOES GREAT EVERY WEEK AND RELATIONSHIPS WITHIN THE GROUP ARE FLOURISHING, BUT NO CHANGES OCCUR IN MEMBERS' LIVES, THERE'S A PROBLEM.

UNDER CONSTRUCTION

We live in a day when people find it easy to talk about being a Christian, yet act differently than what they claim to believe. Almost 50 percent of college students would call themselves "religious," with 22 percent claiming to be "born again." Why don't we see this reflected more on campus?

Small groups can sometimes be part of the problem of unapplied knowledge rather than the solution. Groups can talk about the Bible, engage in theological discussions, but still ignore the critical step of applying God's truth to their lives. As a small group leader your job is to create an environment which promotes application and encourages life-change. Unless the content makes the twelve-inch jump from their heads to their hearts and into their lives, your group hasn't yet learned the truth of God's Word. They'll walk away unchanged.

Our generation is not the first to struggle with matching behavior with beliefs. James questions those who claim to believe, yet act differently (James 2:14-26). The apostle John writes, "Whoever claims to live in Him must walk as Jesus did" (1 John 2:6). Jesus said, "He who has my commandments and obeys them, he is the one who loves me" (John 14:21). True belief results in application.

5.1

52

CHANGING AT THE HEART LEVEL

Last chapter we discussed the difference between surface needs and heart-level needs. As a Bible study leader, it's critical that you understand the surface needs of your group members. But if you stop there you will have missed the mark of helping your group experience genuine life-change.

1 *The sin beneath the behavior: our Fallen Condition.*

You were introduced in the last chapter to a girl who was sleeping with her boyfriend, a guy using pornography, and a new believer struggling with alcohol. You were also introduced to Bible Bob and Sally Sanctification. Let's throw into the mix, Honor Roll Harry.

Everyone likes Harry. He's adored by his professors, doesn't skip class, turns in his assignments on time, even makes time for activities like going to your Bible study: what's not to like? But Honor Roll Harry may be a performance junkie, getting a high with every 'A' on his report card. At the heart level, Honor Roll Harry may be motivated by the same things as the guy struggling with alcohol—love, acceptance and ultimately happiness.

Our goal in life is to find acceptance and love. Whatever our peer group defines as 'lovable,' well that's the standard we'll perform to. But why?

Blaise Pascal, said, "All men seek happiness. This is without exception. Whatever different means they employ, they all tend to this end. The cause of some going to war, and of others avoiding it, is the same desire in both, attended with different views. The [human] will never takes the least step but to this object. This is the motive of every action of every man, even of those who hang themselves" (Section VII of *Penses*). In other words, the alcoholic drinks with the same motivation that the performance junkie performs—to be happy.

For some, their heart-level motivation unconsciously says, "If I perform to this standard I will be somebody (i.e. valuable, acceptable, lovable), and then I'll be happy." For others it might say, "I'm so miserable (i.e. lonely, isolated, unloved) I just want to avoid the pain." And so, they escape by using drugs, pornography, and yes, even religion.

There's a term for this drive and desire; it's called our Fallen Condition. Our Fallen Condition is any motivation that seeks to find life, love, and acceptance apart from Christ, as a substitute for Christ. And so, as you look around your group, while manifested in different behaviors, realize that every single person—as well as yourself—shares the same heart condition: a sinful inclination to find life outside of a relationship with Christ.

53

GARY'S HONESTY

My group leader was seriously dating someone, and we routinely gave him a hard time about it. We were thrilled when he told us he was engaged. However, a few months later he told us that she had broken the engagement. He could have left it at that, but over the next few months he was quite open with his hurt feelings and his effort to trust God in the situation. His honesty really brought our group closer to him and each other. We found out he didn't always know why God did things either. It was a great experience for our group.

Let's look at an example of how to expose the heart condition from a Bible passage. Imagine you are reading the book of James and you come across the following verse: "Come now, you who say, 'Today or tomorrow we will go into such and such a town and spend a year there and trade and make a profit'—yet you do not know what tomorrow will bring. What is your life? For you are a mist that appears for a little time and then vanishes. Instead you ought to say, 'If the Lord wills, we will live and do this or that.' As it is, you boast in your arrogance. All such boasting is evil" (James 4:13-16).

In this passage James appears to criticize all attempts to plan for the future. If we start by asking, "What should I do?" then we may try to identity situations in which planning for the future is wrong. But in doing this we may entirely miss James's point. In fact, we would. If, however, we ask the question "What does this reveal about my brokenness that requires Christ's work in my life?" then we are in a better position to discern James's true purpose.

Notice the reference to "boast" and "boasting" in the passage. James is speaking to a prideful spirit of independence that says, "I'm the master of my fate, the controller of my destiny." James invites us to come to the Lord acknowledging our propensity to control our future and live independently from him. What I hear Christ saying is "Entrust your future to me," not merely "Stop making boastful claims about your future, you braggart." This kind of trust requires a renovation of my soul.

2 *How The Passage Points To Christ.*

We are now on our way to understanding how people change. Once you move from outward behavior to heart level motivations and inclinations, you are taking the first steps to leading your group to life-change. But there is a second question we need to ask. The Scripture doesn't leave us to simply wallow in our sin, so neither should you leave your group there. After we've asked, "What does this reveal about my brokenness that requires the work of Christ?" we next must ask, "How does this passage point me to Christ?" In doing so we are looking to our relationship with Christ for a solution.

The passage may lead us to experience Christ in the following ways: 1. Experiencing the purifying forgiveness of Christ; 2. Experiencing the purifying power of Christ; and 3. Experiencing the purifying promises of Christ.

Experiencing the purifying forgiveness of Christ means that on the one hand I increasingly realize the depth of my sinfulness before God; while on the other hand, because of what Christ has done for me, I increasingly comprehend what it means to be totally and unconditionally loved by God. Tim Keller, pastor of Redeemer Church in New York City puts it this way, "[the gospel] tells us that we are more wicked than we ever dared believe, but more loved and accepted than you ever dared hope—at the same time."

This experience of grace and forgiveness is dramatically illustrated in Luke 7:36-50. A sinful woman erupts with joy as Jesus wipes her sins away, to the visible displeasure of a Pharisee named Simon. Simon doesn't get grace. Simon doesn't get Jesus. And so Jesus explains it to him: "Therefore, I tell you, her many sins have been forgiven — for she loved much. But he who

55

CHRIS' BURNING SINS

One night my small group was studying forgiveness and I wanted to illustrate 1 John 1:9. We wrote out our sins on pieces of paper and went out behind the dorm to set them on fire. Well, the security guards came and broke up our confessional. Did I commit a sin while trying to illustrate forgiveness?

CHRISTINE'S PRAYER CARDS

I had five girls in my group, and I made a prayer card for each of them. Some of the things I wrote on it were things they asked me to pray for and some were things I wanted to see God do in their lives. Often I prayed through Bible passages like Ephesians 1 or Colossians 1. Every Monday I carried my "Lisa" card that had Lisa's prayer requests on it and throughout the day I would pray for her. Tuesday was Kari's day, etc. It was good for me to begin to pray consistently, and they were blessed as God answered my prayers. Something worked because it's been more than ten years since that time and all five women are still walking with God.

has been forgiven little loves little"(Luke 7:47). The difference between Simon the Pharisee and the sinful woman was not the amount of their sin. It was that the woman accurately perceived the depth of her sin and as a result experienced the full measure of the grace given to her.

As you begin to uncover the Fallen Condition within the hearts of your group members, they will need to experience afresh the healing grace and

SANDRA'S HUG

Beth was in my small group her freshman year, and I was really looking forward to seeing her after her first summer at home. When I saw her across the union during orientation week, I ran up to her to give her a big hug. She was pretty cool toward me, as she had already made up her mind to not come back to our group this year. I knew my best shot was to at least get her to drop by our first group. She did, and when she realized how much the other women cared about her, she changed her mind. The next year she was ready to lead her own group.

forgiveness of Christ. The more we understand (know and feel) our wicked-ness, the more we can understand (know and feel) grace.

Experiencing the purifying power of Christ means that, not only does He cleanse us from the guilt of sin, He provides freedom from the power of sin. The gospel is not simply good news because we've been forgiven for our sin but it's good news because God has provided power through his indwelling Spirit: power, as the apostle Paul states in Ephesians 3:14-19, to comprehend the breadth and length and height and depth of the love of Christ; and power, as Romans 8 declares, to walk in righteousness. So, as you lead your group point their eyes to the life-changing power that can only be found in Christ.

Finally, *experiencing the purifying promises of Christ* means that your group members experience hope. Hope, in the biblical sense of the word, ac-tually means assurance: it is assurance that produces hope within us. There are many promises found in Scripture of which we can be assured and take comfort in, all of which are grounded in Christ. Take for example Hebrews 13:5, which says, "I will never leave you nor forsake you." That's a promise! Our assurance in this promise yields hope and security. In Christ, the prom-ises go on and on and on: promises of empowerment, healing, answered prayer, et cetera. As you lead your group, seek to point them to the promises that best address their true and felt need.

3 Responding to Christ.

The application aspect of the Bible study, then, is more of a response than a list of 5 things the group needs to do. It is initially a response to God's Word as it searches our hearts and convicts us of our brokenness, of the ways in which we seek to find life apart from Christ. And then it is a response to Christ: choosing to run to Him for cleansing, forgiveness, love, security, and whatever else our heart is ultimately looking for in sin.

Leading a group toward life-change isn't something you add on to your group; it's the focus of your group. Pray for life-change. Work toward it. Expect it. Model it. Build it into your group. Don't become so enthralled with orchestrating an excellent discussion that you lose sight of the goal of responding to God, which is what leads to life-change.

5.2

57

PRAYING FOR YOUR GROUP

One of the most important things you can do as a group leader is pray fervently for the individuals in your group. There are no tricks to this. It's simply a matter of asking God to work powerfully in their lives. Ultimately, God is the one who changes a person, as Paul wrote, "I planted the seed, Apollos watered it, but God made it grow" (1 Corinthians 3:6).

If God doesn't change the people in your group, they'll never change. So, if God is the key ingredient for life-change to occur, it makes sense that prayer plays a critical role in helping others change.

RAY'S REQUEST

My small group leader told us he wasn't enjoying God's Word and was having trouble spending time in it every day. So he asked us to ask him about it the next week, and he told us he would ask us as well. That next week he had great times in the Word, and so did we.

MARY'S HARD CONFRONTATION

One of the hardest things I ever had to do as a group leader was confront one of the members about habitual lying. She would lie about even the littlest things that didn't even matter. I dreaded the day I finally talked to her. Maybe no one had ever loved her enough to confront her before.

Often Paul and Jesus were found praying for those they led. Study these prayers to learn more about praying for those in your group. Pray through the prayers for those in your group. In Colossians 1:9-12, Paul prays for the believers in Colossae, asking God to fill them with the knowledge of His will so that

KAREN'S DECISION

One of the women in my group had been involved in Campus Crusade for four years. She was a leader in the ministry, and many students looked to her to set the pace. She started dating a non-Christian guy, and we all knew it wasn't a good situation.

At first she told me it was no big deal because they were just friends. Then as they fell in love, she began to rationalize his lack of spiritual maturity. I finally got to the point where I felt she shouldn't be a part of our discipleship group anymore because she was deliberately going against God's design for a relationship.

I think she hated me for awhile, but a couple of weeks later, although she still really loved him, she broke up with him. Not too long after, she met a great Christian guy, they went bonkers over each other, and got married. Confronting her was tough but worth it!

58

they may live lives worthy of God and bear fruit. Jesus prays for His disciples in John 17:6-19 and asks the Father to protect and sanctify them.

Prayer is often a forgotten aspect of leading a group. Carve out regular time to ask God to change every person, including you, in the group. You can plan, teach, and pray for life-change, but there's one more element that will greatly influence your group: it's the encouragement and modeling of those in your group who walk with the Lord and who help others do likewise.

5.3

LOOKING OUT FOR ONE ANOTHER

When people care for others, they begin to look out for one another. As a result, each person in the group grows stronger from the influence of others. Solomon wrote, "As iron sharpens iron, so one man sharpens another" (Proverbs 27:17).

A small group can provide positive encouragement—a healthy sense of peer pressure. When individuals in your group are around others in the group who are taking steps to honor God, it will have a refining effect. Christian students need each other for accountability, encouragement and help in facing the many temptations of the world around them.

As you gain experience leading a group, you'll likely observe firsthand how a group can provide powerful encouragement for those in it to take the next step in their relationship with the Lord. Struggling believers often pull through because their group encourages them and models that it can be done.

On the other hand, when individuals make a deliberate choice to rebel against God, they'll almost always come less often to the group. It's too difficult for them to live one life and be intimately involved in a group where others are living a different lifestyle.

There are several things you can do as a leader to help the group begin to care and look out for each other. Developing a sense of responsibility for each other in the group will take time, and it occurs naturally as the group gets to know each other.

Here are a few suggestions to help you as a leader:

First, set the example by acknowledging you need the support and encouragement of the group. Ask them to pray for an area in which you are struggling (be appropriate with what you share). Be part of the group, admit your need for encouragement, and give it to those in your group. As group members see your example, they'll follow.

Second, have the courage to talk to individuals in your group if they are obviously living contrary to God's Word. Do this humbly and graciously, not as one who is perfect, but rather as one striving to please the Lord. Avoid a judgmental or harsh attitude. As a group leader you'll inevitably encounter situations like this. You can choose to ignore these situations, which is an easy but unloving

59

RANDY'S RESPONSIBILITY

Brad came to my group sporadically for a couple of years, usually when he had no other conflicts. Eventually he quit coming to group. One day we ran into each other and he asked me to call him every week to remind him of the Campus Crusade meeting. After four years he still was looking to me to get him to the Campus Crusade meeting. I told him I'd gladly remind him when I saw him, but he needed to begin to take responsibility for his own relationship with God.

alternative, or you can lovingly go to the person to see if you can help. Solomon wrote, "Wounds from a friend can be trusted, but an enemy multiplies kisses" (Proverbs 27:6).

It's important for the leader and those in the group to realize they have a responsibility toward each other. This is healthy, as God has clearly taught us that we should love each other, admonish one another, bear one another's burdens, etc. These are responsibilities we have toward each other. But this is different than being responsible for those in the group.

For example, if someone in the group is ac-tively involved in some kind of immoral behavior, believers around that person have a responsibil-ity to talk to that person and offer help. But they aren't responsible to change that person's behav-ior. That's the individual's decision. Some very unhealthy relationships can develop when people feel the need to take responsibility for another per-son's life.

Third, have the group commit itself to encour-aging one another to live lives which honor the Lord. You might say something like, "It's difficult to live the Christian life without the help of others. In this group one of the things we'll want to do is help each other live God-honoring lives. So every week we'll talk about how to practically apply the Scriptures to our lives, as well as talk about ways we can encourage one another to do the same."

Fourth, encourage those in your group to take responsibility for their lives. You can point them to the Lord, but they need to make their own deci-sions and learn to honor the Lord in their lives.

Planning a Bible study lesson is one thing: you study the passage, apply it in your own life, think of some personal illustrations, and write questions that create great discussion. But application for your group members is another matter. You can't control it. You can pray for it, model it, teach toward it, and encourage it, but you can't make it happen. A wise leader takes responsibility for his part and understands where his responsibilities end. Whether your group members apply God's Word is not your responsibility. When things go well, tell God. When you are discouraged, tell God. Either way, remember that God causes the growth..

Too often today people blame others for their poor choices. You do your group members a great favor by telling them you and the group can be a resource, but it's their life. You can encourage this by saying things such as, "Well, it's your life Scott. What do you think God wants you to do about this passage?" or, "That's a tough choice. What are the pro's and con's? What do you think the Lord wants you to do?" Help them make decisions for themselves.

CONCLUSION

In this chapter we've talked about promoting life-change and looking out for one another. These two issues are obviously related. As the group learns to look out for each other, it will help individuals make changes in their lives. Likewise, as you establish the importance of applying God's Word, they'll feel an increased need to help each other act on what they've learned. Both of these areas are crucial to a small group.

One of the greatest challenges you'll probably face is helping promote application. It's far easier to just have a good discussion. However, as you've had pounded into your head in this chapter, a group that doesn't bring about life-change falls short of all God wants it to be.

61

FOR THOUGHT / DISCUSSION

1 Have you ever been around someone who would talk one way but live another? What was your view of that person? How did it affect you?

2 Have you ever been in a group that had a refining effect on your behavior? What was it like?

3 Agree or disagree: "Most small groups strongly emphasize content, but tend to come up short in the application portion." If you agree, why do you think this so? In your opinion, what are the keys to directing a small group toward life-change?

4 Has there ever been a time when another believer lovingly confronted you about an issue? If so, how did you feel? How did you respond? If not, how do you think your life might be different if someone had done so?

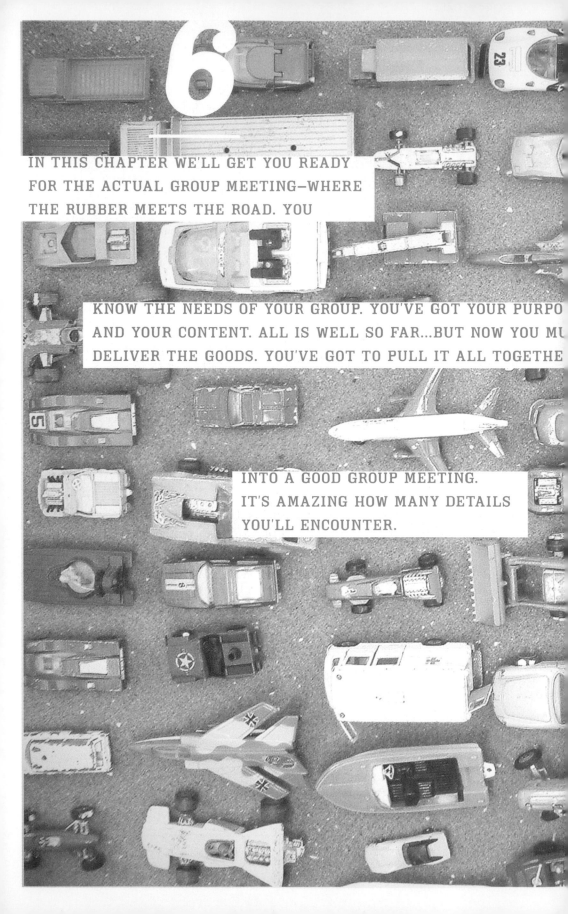

6

IN THIS CHAPTER WE'LL GET YOU READY FOR THE ACTUAL GROUP MEETING—WHERE THE RUBBER MEETS THE ROAD. YOU

KNOW THE NEEDS OF YOUR GROUP. YOU'VE GOT YOUR PURPO AND YOUR CONTENT. ALL IS WELL SO FAR...BUT NOW YOU MU DELIVER THE GOODS. YOU'VE GOT TO PULL IT ALL TOGETHE

INTO A GOOD GROUP MEETING. IT'S AMAZING HOW MANY DETAILS YOU'LL ENCOUNTER.

YOUR GROUP WON'T KNOW THE TOIL
YOU'VE PUT INTO PREPARING, BUT THEY'LL
SURE NOTICE WHAT HAPPENS COME

TUESDAY NIGHT (OR WHENEVER). GROUP
MEMBERS WILL DECIDE WHETHER THEY'LL
RETURN BASED ON WHAT GOES ON IN THE

ACTUAL GROUP, SO
BE PREPARED...

HITTING THE ROAD

6.1

PREPARING THE LESSON

There are two important phases to preparing a lesson:

First: Apply the lesson yourself.
You can't lead a good discussion and point a group toward life changing application if you haven't studied and applied it yourself.

Study the lesson, asking God to teach you from His Word. Consider how the passage exposes our brokenness. Ask God to show you how he wants you to respond to Christ through what you are learning. If you're personally involved with the material, you'll find it easier to provide personal illustrations.

Second: Discover the big idea of the lesson.
Go back through it and think about how to help the group discover and apply the truths of the lesson. Here are four steps that will help you prepare to lead the lesson.

1 Pray.

No matter how confident you feel in your ability to lead a group, continually ask God to guide you in your planning and implementation. You can plant a seed and water it, but God must cause the growth. You can prepare a brilliant lesson, but God must change lives. Spend time asking God to change you and the people in your group. Ask Him for wisdom and direction as you prepare. It's possible to spend hours preparing for your group time, but bottom line, it's God who uses His Word and Spirit to work in and through you.

2 Discover the big idea.

After you've spent some time studying the passage, summarize the big idea of your passage in a single sentence. "I think the big idea of this passage is _____."

3 Determine the learning objectives for the lesson.

In light of what this passage is saying, answer the following questions: "What do I want them to understand and believe? What do I want them to experience? How do I want them to respond to Christ? (Be sure your application is aimed at heart-resistance to Christ.)

Write down your answers to 2 and 3 at the start of the lesson. This will help you focus your questions and allocate your time around the key objectives of the study.

4 Go through the lesson and choose good questions.

Select questions and activities that will help group members discover and apply the truths of the lesson. Think of specific examples you can share from your own life. Focus the lesson on the objectives you determined in step 3. Keep in mind that you want them discover and apply the truth themselves.

In Chapter 8, you'll learn how to ask good questions that target the heart and direct the discussion toward your group members experiencing Christ and real life-change.

After you get a good grasp on the lesson, you can choose the various elements which make up your meeting, such as icebreakers (relationship-building activities) and prayer.

6.2

PLANNING YOUR GROUP SESSION

Several questions may come to mind as you plan the group session: What elements should I include in the group this week? How long should I spend on each element, such as the lesson, prayer, fellowship, etc.? How can I best structure the group session to meet the needs of those in the group?

Think about a small group you liked. What made it enjoyable? Your leader probably did some fun things to help members get to know each other. You might have spent time praying. You studied the Bible. You might have gone somewhere together as a group. Think through these issues as you determine what to include in each group session:

- What is the purpose of this group?

67

- What are the needs of this group?

- What are you trusting God to do in this group?

- How does this specific group session fit your overall purpose?

MARK'S NOT-SO-BRILLIANT PLAN

The University of North Carolina is a beautiful, sprawling campus, but it's also a 20-minute walk over hilly terrain from end to end. When I wanted to start a Bible study we used a survey to find fifty guys who were interested. I had this brilliant plan of how to save time and make the Bible study more convenient for me.

I didn't have the time to visit all these guys, so I just dropped notes in their mailboxes. I set the meeting for 8 on Sunday night because that's when I had free time. I also thought it would be most convenient to meet in a classroom close by. Boy, was I wrong. When I showed up the first week, I found I had also saved a lot of other people time: only three of the fifty guys showed up that night.

I talked to Shannon, my leader, and he helped me take a different approach. That next week we visited many of the fifty students and changed the meeting time to a weekday. Plus we moved the location to a meeting room in their residence hall. I was encouraged when fifteen guys showed up. I learned my lesson to make things convenient for the guys, not me.

In light of your conclusions, select elements for this group time that will help facilitate your purpose and objectives. After you've selected the elements, determine the time allotment for each element.

Let's consider a small group that has been together for only five weeks. Many of the women know each other from the soccer team. The group leader decides the group session would include a time for interaction with each other (15 minutes), time in the Word (35 minutes), prayer (5 minutes) and announcements (5 minutes). What might happen in each of these four sections?

Components of a Small Group Meeting

1 Interaction with each other.

This is relationship-building time. It may include icebreakers or some other form of sharing time or fellowship. A relationship building time is crucial for any group, even if group members know each other. The leader can use a question, or icebreaker, that will help everyone get to know each other better. It's important for the leader to choose an activity that fits into the time allotted for fellowship. Chapter 6 discusses the importance of building relationships within the group and gives many specific icebreakers and ideas for group interaction.

Never underestimate the importance of creating an atmosphere where people feel at home. Icebreakers or other relational interaction are great for this, and you'll find that food always helps.

68

KELLI'S LEADER

Jeanine led the Bible study I was in at Michigan State. The first meeting was fun, but she just wasn't clicking with us during our second meeting. Jeanine had been so intent on teaching the Bible that she hadn't taken time to listen to what we were saying, so we didn't share personal stuff. Plus she wasn't really telling us much about herself.

The next time we met, however, she began the group by talking about some of the fears she experienced the first time she was in a small group Bible study. I could relate to how she hid her Bible on the way to her first Bible study and how she'd always explain to her friends that she was going to study at the library. Jeanine's honesty broke the ice. One girl told them about how her older sister had always warned her to stay away from anything religious. Another girl talked about her doubts about the Bible's truthfulness, something I thought about sometimes. That Bible study helped me get a lot of my questions answered because Jeanine took the time to be vulnerable.

Food is power, they say. It communicates to your group that you went out of your way for them. It also makes people feel more comfortable. Jesus taught 90 percent of the time in the context of a meal.

2 Interaction with God's Word.

This is when the group studies and applies God's Word together. Most leaders see this as the real meat of the group. Interaction with the Word is central, but sometimes the other sections of the group session make the time in the Word come alive.

CAUTION
Icebreakers can run long. If you don't watch it, your group will be one big icebreaker. This isn't all bad at times, but it might communicate to some in your group that you don't value the lesson portion of the your group meeting very much. Maybe they'll think it isn't worth the time to come. You're better off guiding the discussion and planning ahead so you can control the length of the icebreaker.

JESSICA'S COOKIES
I wasn't a Christian when I was invited to my first Bible study. My leader brought cookies to that first group. The next week I came back primarily for the cookies and they kept me coming. I guess you could say God used cookies to lead me to Christ (indirectly, of course).

TOM'S "GOODS"
My discipleship group at Auburn University included four young men—Paul, Hank, John and Matt. Each week we took turns bringing "the goods"—the pop and junk food of choice. Food always brings a sense of community... especially IBC Root Beer in bottles.

3 Interaction with God in prayer.

Spend time praying. As a group grows together, prayer increases in importance. A new group usually won't feel comfortable praying together. So, you can share briefly about prayer, discussing why we pray or how to pray. Give them time to warm up to group prayer. You could pray for the group meeting and maybe ask a more mature member to pray at the end of the meeting. In the appendix you'll find some ideas on how to teach your group to pray.

Some groups, even though they are made up of young believers, enjoy sharing prayer requests with each other. This helps the group bond together and helps their faith grow as they see God's answers. The prayer time might

RANDY'S DISTRACTIONS

I remember the first small group meeting I attended. There was a guy named John, but I never really got to know him because he always sat on his loft. All I saw was the bottom of his Nikes. No one talked. The leader seemed like his mind was on the Bulls' game blaring from the TV in the corner. I was always thinking, How can I get out of this? When the phone rang, I wanted it to be my roommate with some "emergency" which only I could take care of. The material the leader gave us made great doodling paper. I could hardly wait to get out of there.

SUSAN'S SURPRISE SICKNESS

I was leading a sorority Bible study at Clemson. It was our first study and I wanted to make the women feel special, so I made a pie. About ten minutes after eating her slice, one of the women in the study started grabbing her stomach saying, "I don't feel so good." She ran from the room and threw up. I found out later it was something else she ate earlier, but the girls must have been thinking, What is this woman giving us?

70

become the group's favorite time.

4 Information about upcoming activities.

This lets your group know what's happening in the ministry so they'll have opportunities to meet new people. In this portion you communicate any details about events going on during the next week or two—the campus weekly meeting, any upcoming activities in the ministry, clarify the meeting time for the next week. You might suggest someone bring the goodies or get a volunteer to help with an icebreaker.

You should always include a teaser for next week's topic to motivate them to come back. For example, "Next week we're going to look at what to do when we blow it in our Christian life" or, "Next week we'll look at biblical guidelines for dating."

Each ingredient helps produce an effective small group, but they won't always be exhibited to the same degree each time your group meets.

An older group might spend more time in the Word and in prayer than a younger group: 60 percent interaction with God's Word, 20 percent interaction with each other, 15 percent interaction with God, 5 percent information about upcoming activities.

These examples aren't perfect models because there is no "right" combination of elements. The leader must make each group session fit the purpose and needs of the group. Sometimes the sessions won't always work out like you planned.

The crucial point in planning your group time is to wisely structure each element to help meet the needs of your group members. A staff member or veteran group leader can help you make wise choices.

6.3

DESIGNING THE RIGHT ENVIRONMENT

A key element to every group is the mood or tone. What happens apart from the content helps to enhance (or sometimes destroy) your group members' experiences. Some groups seem to soar, partly because of a comfortable environment.

71

THE PAUSE THAT REFRESHES
There are times when the women in my Bible study are really struggling or discouraged. On days like this sometimes we spend more time sharing prayer requests and encouraging each other to trust God. When I take time to meet their needs, it shows I care about them. The women really appreciate these times.

LORI'S OFFERING
I was holding the second meeting of a new Bible study with some women at Louisiana Tech. In the first meeting I had told the girls they could pay for their Bible study books at the next meeting. One of the girl's first visit to the group was at the second meeting. She arrived late just as the girls were passing their three dollars for the books to me. The meeting time ended and as this girl left she pressed a couple dollar bills into my hand and said, "Thank you." I guess she thought we had just collected an offering.

Jesus knew the influence of environment in learning. He taught about the resurrection outside the tomb of Lazarus and about His identity amid the natural beauty of Caesarea Philippi. He taught about prayer in the Garden of

Gethsemane, about faith in a boat, righteous anger in the temple, and evangelism beside a dusty well in a Samaritan village. Each change in environment brought an opportunity to teach another truth. (Don't take this too far. You don't have to move your group every week to match your topic.)

Think about the atmosphere you'll be creating in your small group. Ask yourself, "What can I do to communicate to my group that this is a safe place

Bad Environments for Small Groups
- *Your roommate's "Naughty Cheerleaders of the Big Ten" poster makes the guys drool like leaky faucets.*
- *The phone rings regularly during the group. When it does, everyone stops talking and listens to the person talking on the phone.*
- *The guys in your afternoon Bible study nod lethargically after coming down from a sugar high brought on by a lunch of Snickers and Mountain Dew.*
- *Your roommate keeps coming in every five minutes, saying, "I just need to grab one more thing, and I promise I won't bother you again."*
- *A local rock group rehearses in the room above you.*
- *The room is so dark and musty that sewer workers regularly walk through wearing those lighted helmets.*
- *The room gets so hot that sometimes the members of your Bible study literally become on fire for the Lord.*

for them to come? How can I help people be comfortable? How do I minimize distractions? What conditions will enhance learning?"

Developing the right environment helps establish a sense of belonging. The environment will influence how people feel about your group, how well they learn, and if they will come back.

Here are some keys to creating a good environment:

- Meet in an informal and accessible location. Often a great place to meet is in the room of a group member as long as it's OK with their roommates. Places such as a church may intimidate new group members. Likewise, classrooms may be familiar and accessible, but they hinder communication and warmth.

- Set your meeting time so that all members are able to attend. Choose a time when your members are likely to be sharp and awake and make sure no one has an ongoing schedule conflict. Friday afternoons and late nights are better for blowing off steam or sleeping than for a small group meeting.

- Arrange the seating so everyone can easily see one another. Sitting in a circle at the same level will help. Also be aware of the distance separating each member. Try to sit close enough so each person has eye contact and can hear one another easily, but not so close people feel uncomfortable or their personal space is being invaded.

- Meet in a location where you can control distractions and interruptions as much as possible. Unplug the phone and turn down the volume on the answering machine. Put a sign on the door to prevent people from knocking. Turn off the TV. It's also not a good idea to meet in a room where outside noise can interfere with your group.

- Provide refreshments (especially in the first few weeks) to help warm up the group and give people something to do at the beginning of the meeting.

BETSY'S FIRST BIBLE STUDY

The first Bible study I went to was pretty good considering I expected the leader to be stuffy. She turned out to be really fun. The study was so interesting that I completely forgot about the biology midterm I had the next day. The warm brownies made up for me missing dinner. I even found myself talking about things I've never shared before. I was really encouraged to walk with God after that and couldn't wait until our next meeting.

JUDY'S HIDE AND GO SEEK

I led a group in my sorority in which we asked at our meeting who would be interested in a Bible study—about fifteen girls said "yes." The biggest frustration was that we averaged three or four each time and they were different people every time. Also, people used to hide on the day of Bible study to avoid me. (By the way, I did the same thing a few years before— hide when I was in my first group.)

- Make sure you have good lighting to create a warm feeling. No one should have to look into the sun or toward a bright window. Likewise, avoid dark, catacomb-type rooms. You are developing fellowship, not film.

- Choose a location where you can freely interact and carry out the content of your small group plan. Make sure you have any equipment you may need.

- Bring extra Bibles. Some group members may forget to bring one or won't have a readable translation.

6.4

TEN SUGGESTIONS FOR THE FIRST GROUP MEETING

The first group meeting is a crucial one. People will sometimes decide whether they will return based on this meeting. It's also a unique meeting since sometimes group members are unfamiliar with each other, you, where to meet, etc. Don't be surprised if your first meeting takes a lot of energy and time to get going. It's worth it to make it a success.

Here are some ideas that will help you start off well:

1 Visit every potential group member prior to the meeting. If you can't visit everyone, a phone call is more effective than a note. Take the time to be personal on the phone—they need more than just a, "Tomorrow night at 8:00." When you drop by, establish a more personal relationship by asking about their photos, posters, classes, major, family, or how their week has been. Help them see their need to be in a group by asking what they want out of this Bible study. Lastly, give them the details: Make sure they know when and where—write it out.

2 Take care of all the details regarding the environment—i.e., the room, time, lighting, etc.

DAN'S MISTAKE

I was leading a Bible study and early on I asked each guy to share his testimony. The first said, "A friend and I were getting high on my front porch when I was in high school. The wind wasn't blowing at all, but I looked up in this tree and saw a small section of leaves moving back and forth, so I knew there must be a God."

I moved on to the next guy, hoping for something better. He said, "I was at a Christian retreat (this looked a little more promising) and was at a dance. There was a girl I liked but she dogged me. I cried and ran down to the lake. I looked up in the sky and said, 'God, if you're up there, give me a sign.' At that moment a shooting star went across the sky." I looked at him and said nothing.

I looked at the last guy with little hope, and he said, "Well, mine is nothing like that. I was at a youth conference and the speaker asked us to come up front to receive Christ, so I went up front and asked Christ into my life." I was sure glad that last guy came through.

3 Be there early to welcome everyone and introduce people to each other. Work like a dog on remembering names.

4 Be enthusiastic, regardless of the turnout. If only one or two people come, you may have to alter your plan and overview some of the material you wanted to cover. Be positive and ask them if they know of anyone else who might be interested. Tell them you are really looking forward to the Bible study.

5 Choose content that will meet needs in the group and can be done in a short time period. Be sure it's non-controversial and easy to teach. You may not want to have a "lesson" the first meeting, preferring to spend time getting to know one another. However, some people might be coming to your group to just check it out, and they expect some time in the Word. If you decide to include content in your first group meeting, discuss some of the biblical principles for growing in faith or for being in a small group.

6 Be careful to plan the actual group time. Give yourself extra time for flexibility so you end on time. You don't want to run long the first group. You might plan your first group something like this:

Sample Schedule for Your First Meeting

- *Introduce yourself. Be personable and real.*   *5 minutes*
- *Pray. You do it. Keep it short.*   *1 minute*
- *Have each member introduce themselves.*   *5 minutes*
- *Icebreaker.*   *20 minutes*
- *Communicate purpose of your group time.*   *5 minutes*
- *Content.*   *15 minutes*
- *Introduce the material, cover details.*   *5 minutes*

7 DON'T put people on the spot by asking for their testimony or having them pray when they aren't prepared to do either. Depending on your group, you can also have some strange conversations that aren't appropriate for the group if you ask too much. Ask safer questions at first.

8 Don't blow people away with your big words, grandiose dreams or spirituality. If you start your freshman group with a lecture on how this group is going to reach the world, you might not have a group left.

9 Be real. Share with the group some of your own journey with the Lord—your ups and downs along the way. Put yourself in their shoes. Remember, they probably don't know what to expect, so help them feel at ease.

10 Be positive when asking people to come each week. You might say something like, "You know, one of the things I'm looking forward to about this group is getting to know each other. If seven of us are here one week and four different people the next, we'll never develop a sense of unity, and we'll never get to know each other. I'll be here every week and hopefully everyone will be able to make this time a priority so we can get to know each other."

Follow up with each person later and ask if they think they can attend the group regularly. Give them room to say "no," but encourage them.

6.5

AFTER YOUR FIRST GROUP MEETING

• Take some time to thank God for your group and the meeting time.

• Try to drop by and see each member at least once before the next meeting to get to know them better and get feedback. You might do something social, but don't force yourself on them. Let them know you care about them as a person.

• For the first couple weeks remind your group about the meeting a day or so before. This can easily be done with a short phone call. After a couple of weeks it will be in their schedule.

FOR THOUGHT / DISCUSSION

1 *Share your first small group experiences. What can you learn, good and bad, from them?*

2 *Agree or disagree: How people feel during and after the first group meeting is more important than what they learn?*

3 *What are some specific steps you can take to create a good atmosphere for your group?*

4 *Does this chapter put you under the pile? If so, in what ways? (For the excessively forlorn and downtrodden, check the "Empty Tank" section again!)*

77

Doesn't it seem like there are a million details to starting a small group? Well, you're right. There is a lot of stuff to think about, to plan, to implement. The things talked about in this lesson are the ideals of helping you get a group together. You can't do everything and things do go wrong. You may run overtime your first meeting or mess up someone's name five times. The conversation might go off on weird tangents. Just relax. Everything doesn't have to be perfect. Trust the Lord, care about your people, and give it your best.

THE YEAR IS 2030. THE GROUP GATHERING IN YOUR HOME IS NOT JUST ANY GROUP—IT'S YOUR OLD PALS FROM YOUR SMALL GROUP IN COLLEGE. IT'S BEEN ONLY FIFTEEN YEARS BUT A FEW KIDS, A FEW POUNDS, AND LESS HAIR SURE HAVE CHANGED HOW EVERYONE LOOKS. BUT THEIR HEARTS ARE THE

SAME. EACH ONE CONTINUES TO WALK WITH GOD AND REMEMBER THE GOOD OLD DAYS. WHAT DO YOU THINK WILL BE THE TOPIC OF CONVERSATION? DO YOU THINK SOMEONE MIGHT RECALL, "I REMEMBER LESSON FIVE ON GOD'S WORD. WHAT A GREAT LESSON!"? DON'T BET ON IT...

7

TRIPMATES–MORE THAN GAS MONEY

Fifteen years later most people will not remember specific lessons but most likely will remember the relationships within the group. Hopefully God's Word changed the lives of those gathered in your home, but undoubtedly, the weekend discussion would be dominated by fond recollections of good times and friendships in the group.

Relationships are the glue that hold small groups together. If they happen, the group not only survives but flourishes. If they don't, the group is short lived.

The Scriptures are full of teaching, advice and admonishment regarding relationships. Solomon writes, "As iron sharpens iron, so one man sharpens another" (Proverbs 27:17). The author of Hebrews commands, "Let us not give up meeting together, as some are in the habit of doing, but let us encourage one another, and all the more as you see the Day approaching" (Hebrews 10:25).

The Bible, research studies, and the personal experiences of scores of small group-leaders confirm: relationships are crucial for learning and spiritual growth. Relationships within a group help move it from being the "leader's group" to "our group." So, as a group leader, work hard to provide an environment where dynamic and encouraging relationships can be developed.

In this chapter we'll offer suggestions on how to build a sense of community by fostering relationships within your group, both between you and the group and among the group members themselves. We'll also provide ideas for icebreakers (relationship-building activities) and fun activities to do as a group. As you use these resources to get started, you'll gain experience in this aspect of small group dynamics and will soon add your own ideas to this list.

7.1

CULTIVATING CAMARADERIE

In many new groups, the members don't know each other well. Meeting new people can be one of the most uncomfortable things a person can experience, except maybe flunking a test or being overdrawn at the bank.

If individuals are anxious about simply attending the group, it will be difficult to get them to study God's Word together or come back. On the other hand, once the group is comfortable with each other, the relationships within the group will help stimulate the study of God's Word.

Initially, the leader is the key ingredient to building cohesiveness among group members. If you wait for the group to come together on its own, it usually won't. You will often need to take steps to create the kind of atmosphere in which committed relationships can flourish. There are six ways you can help create a sense of community and build camaraderie among group members.

1 *Be an involved and caring leader.*

Group members catch and model the attitude of the leader. If the leader is interested in everyone in the group, looks forward to being with them, and genuinely cares about helping the group learn and grow, the members will pick up on his or her attitude—it's contagious. Here are a few ways a leader can demonstrate a caring heart:

• Pay Attention. People want to know they are being listened to when they're speaking. Don't look ahead in your lesson or stare out the window.

- Be Responsive. When a member gives an answer or shares an insight or opinion, don't just nod and go on to the next person. Instead compliment the person or ask a follow-up question to show your interest.

- Value Others' Opinions. Everyone's input and opinions have value. Don't judge what they share and avoid giving pat answers or quick fixes to their problems.

SARAH'S CARE

My group had been together a couple months and the women in the group were becoming friends. We knew Mary Anne's parents were divorced, but one night in group she began to share the painful details. She said she hadn't seen or heard from her mother in two or three years and had no idea where she lived. She retold a very painful conversation when she, her brother and sister tearfully begged their mother not to leave them, but she walked away anyway. Mary Anne was so embarrassed and hurt that she hadn't felt free to tell her story to anyone at school. The group comforted Mary Anne and her vulnerability brought the group closer together. From that night on the women in the group felt they had a safe place to go.

For example, if someone says they are struggling with being homesick don't fire back, "Well, you know you have a friend in God." No one wants pat answers. One of the best ways to show you value someone's opinions is to ask a follow-up question. So, you could ask this person, "In what ways has it been hard?" or, "What do you miss most about home?"

- Encourage Interaction by asking for their input. What do they think? Do they agree? Disagree? Does anyone else have any input?

- Be Real with your group. Laugh with them, share your struggles and victories, and share your life and love for the Lord. Let them be your friends. You don't have to spill your deepest secrets, but let them know you too are a real person who's in the process of becoming like Christ.

- Maintain Confidentiality. If someone shares something confidentially, honor their request and don't share it outside of the group. Ask the rest of the group to do the same. If the group violates this principle, it will seriously deter others from sharing about their lives.

• Work through conflict. Tension in a group discussion is inevitable. Agree to work through any disagreements. You may have to act as a mediator to make sure all points of view are heard.

2 Regularly plan group time for members to tell each other about their lives.

In the initial stages of a group, an icebreaker is a good way to let people share experiences from their lives.

3 Maximize group interaction.

Prepare questions which help the group interact with each other and God's Word. Provide opportunities for the members to state their observations and thoughts about what they're learning from the Bible. As group members interact with each other it will help facilitate self-discovered learning.

4 Show tangible concern for those in your group.

84

At the end of the group you could ask if anyone has a need for which they would like the group to pray. Perhaps it is a need that you, or the group, could help meet. When people begin to share about their lives, it draws a group together. As group members pray for one another, their concern grows. (Note: Young believers might be hesitant and feel apprehensive at first, but a group will most likely pray more as its members grow and feel more comfortable with one another. See the appendix on how to teach a group to pray.)

5 Do something together as a group outside of the normal meeting time.

Group activities are great for building unity in the group. Even something as simple as going to Starbucks or sitting together at a football game can help a group bond together. Involving a group in some kind of outreach can also unify a group (see Chapter 10).

6 Do activities with individual group members outside your group time.

As group members become more comfortable with you outside of group, they'll be more open and honest inside the group. The third section of this chapter will have some ideas on building relationships with your group members outside of group.

7.2

CREATIVE ICEBREAKERS

Icebreakers encourage people to get to know each other. It is important that icebreakers be non-threatening. What is non-threatening to some group members could terrify others. For example, the question, "Who would you like to go on vacation with for one week and why?", would be threatening to many groups. However, the question, "If you could go on vacation anywhere, where would you go?" is not as threatening.

Here are some suggested icebreakers. The first few are easiest and most helpful for a beginning group. Many of the later ideas are useful for building relationships in groups that have been together for awhile.

1 Best / Worst

Have each person share their best and worst moments from the previous week. Try to steer your group away from school items. It can get boring to hear, "My best was an A in calculus, and my worst was a D in biology." This icebreaker is an easy one to use at first and gives you good feedback concerning their life at the moment. Some veteran groups do this every week. Their bests and worsts will become more honest.

2 Most Unique

Go around the room and have each person share something that makes them different from anyone in the group, like, "I've never left the state I was born in" or, "I am one of ten kids."

3 Two Truths and a Lie

Have each person make three statements about themselves: two true statements and one lie. For example, "I've never broken a bone. I have five sisters. I was born in Yugoslavia." The group tries to guess which statement is the lie.

4 Personal Scavenger Hunt

Take five minutes and find the following items in your wallet or purse—something that: •You've had a long time. •You're proud of. •Reveals a lot about you. •Reminds you of a fun time. •Concerns or worries you.

Have each person share the first item. Go around again on the second item, and again until you have gone through each one. Don't feel like you have to use the whole list because it may take too long.

RACHEL'S BESTS & WORSTS

When I started my group we always did "Bests and Worsts." Usually the women gave safe answers, such as, "My best was a date to the football game." As their sense of community deepened, we kept doing Bests and Worsts, but their answers were more personal. One week after Christmas break, Tracy said her worst was that her parents told her she could never read her Bible in their house again. Her best was the peace she felt from the Lord during this difficult time. Whenever anything good or bad happened during the week the women would remember it, wanting to tell the group the next week. Bests and Worsts were a highlight every week.

CHRISTINE'S PIZZA

I had a pizza party with my girls. When the pizza got there I put a toothpick flag on each slice. On each flag I wrote a "getting to know you" question. Each slice you picked had a question to answer! It was a great icebreaker!

5 Get to Know You Questions

- What do you do for fun?
- What would be your ideal vacation?
- What is the most memorable activity you did with your family when you were a child?
- What quality do you appreciate most in a friend?
- What is one characteristic you received from your parents that you want to keep, and one you wish you could change?
- What is a good thing happening in your life right now? What makes it good?
- If you knew you couldn't fail and money was no object, what would you like to do in the next five years?
- What would you like said at your funeral?
- When, if ever, did God become more than a word to you, and how did it happen?

6 Did You Know?

This is great for a group that doesn't know each other well. Find interesting facts about individual group members before the group meets. Try to discover information that sets each person apart from the others, such as "I have a tugboat named after me" or, "I once wrecked the same quarter panel of my car four times" or, "I have a twin." Then make a sheet with one fact from each person and a blank beside this fact. Give everyone in the group a sheet and five to seven minutes to find who goes in each blank. When they find the right person they must also learn one other fact about that person. At the end, introduce everyone in the group in the order on the list.

7 Chart Your Life

Thinking back as far as you can, draw a line graph to represent your life. Consider the high points, the low points, moments of inspiration, moments of despair, leveling off times, and where you are now. The line will probably be a mixture of straight, slanted, jagged and curved lines. After you've drawn it, share what it means to you with the group.

8 M&M's Game

Pass a bag of M&M's around and tell everyone to take a few. Then, before they eat them ask them to share something for every M&M. For example, something about their family for every red one, something about their plans for the future for every green one, etc.

> **STAN'S BOWLING**
> *Our Bible study went bowling with a group of women on some old-fashioned lanes where we had to set up our own pins. We took turns in the back setting up the pins. It was a riot. Afterwards we all went back to our leader's room at the fraternity house for dessert. It was a great bonding time because it was the first thing we'd done as a group outside of the regular meeting.*

9 Most Deprived

Buy a large bag of M&M's and give each person the same amount (try ten M&Ms). Start by stating something you've never done that you think everyone else has done (thus the name "Most Deprived"). For example, you might say, "I've never had a birthday party," or some other true statement about yourself that you think everyone else has surely done. Then, everyone who has had a birthday party pays you an M&M. You pay everyone who has not had a party. Keep playing until everyone has a turn or until someone runs out of M&M's. Obviously the idea is to come up with the most M&M's and be most deprived. This activity will take more time.

10 You Write the Question

Give each person a 3x5 card. You pick the topic and let them write the questions. For example, you choose "friendship" as a topic, and they each write out a question for anyone in the group to answer about friendship. For example, "What do you value most in a friend?" or, "Who was your best friend growing up and why?" Then pile all the cards face down in the middle of the group and let people draw.

You can do this for weeks by changing the topic. Topic ideas on the lighter side: jobs, life goals, funny stories, hobbies, etc. Topic ideas on the more vulnerable side: family, fears, dating issues, significant relationships, relationship with God, etc.

11 My Life in Pictures

Bring a newspaper or magazine. Have each person tear out a picture, article or anything they think tells something about themselves. If there's enough time they can make a collage that tells more about themselves.

12 House on Fire

Ask, "Your house is on fire, and everyone is safe. You have thirty seconds to run through the house and collect three or four articles you want to save. What would you grab? Why?" After everyone has done this, the group can discuss what they learned about the things they value.

13 Make Believe

If you could go anywhere in the world now, where would you go and why? If you could talk to anyone in the world, who would it be? Why? If you could talk to any person who has died, who would you talk to and why? If you could wish one thing to come true about your upcoming summer, what would it be?

14 Deserted Island

Ask, "You've been exiled to a deserted island for a year. You are told you may take three things you want, apart from the essentials. What would you take and why?"

15 Spiritual Journey

After the group has been together for awhile, take turns sharing your testimonies and discussing your spiritual pilgrimage.

16 Heroes

Ask each member to name three people, past or present, they admire. Why? Or, ask them if they could interview anyone in history, who would that be and why? What one or two questions would you want to ask?

7.3

DEVELOPING RELATIONSHIPS

If you want to be an effective small group leader, you need to know your job doesn't stop after the group meeting is over. The small group meeting is a structured, time-limited activity that's focused primarily on learning and applying God's Word. A sense of belonging and community can be developed in such an environment, but it has its limits. Involvement with members outside the official small group session is crucial for significant relationships to develop.

89

Roles

There are several different roles you may play as you make friends with those in your group. Foremost, be sure you are a friend to them, someone with whom they feel they can be themselves and enjoy. You must therefore make

JARVIS' FRIEND

I wasn't very faithful in attending my first group as a freshman at Ole Miss. Brad, my leader, continued to come by and spend time with me. His commitment to our relationship influenced me a great deal more than he would have imagined. Over the last four years, Brad has become my closest friend.

TOM'S GREAT FRIENDSHIP

I was in Ralph's group at the University of South Carolina. He would meet with Tom, Jimmy and me to talk about what God was doing in our lives or share Christ with friends on campus. On Saturday mornings we'd hang around his dorm room and pray about anything and everything for a couple of hours. Ralph was much more than just my small group leader, he was a great friend. In fact, he was the first person outside of my family that told me that he loved me.

sure you are not condescending or aloof. Initiate with them and enjoy being with them.

A second role you may play is that of an older sister/brother. Older sisters and brothers tend to look out for the younger siblings. Younger siblings also tend to come to older brothers and sisters for advice. This is a relationship you can't force, just like you can't get your younger brother to do what you want him to do. Hopefully, over time those in your group will come to you for help.

You will also play the role of a coach at times. A coach instructs, but also cheers on his team. Everyone needs a little encouragement. A pat on the back or communicating respect when they make good decisions will go far.

BENEFITS OF BUILDING RELATIONSHIPS OUTSIDE THE GROUP

* *You can identify and meet their needs.*

* *They'll begin to see you, not as just their group leader, but as a friend.*

* *God's Word comes alive as you live it out practically day-to-day before them.*

* *Informal times together builds trust.*

* *Character and depth builds as you discuss truth and deal with life and each other in a natural, non-structured setting.*

MELVITA'S RAID
I was in a women's Bible study and we decided to bust into guy's Bible study with care packages. We wanted to encourage them in their walks and have some fun.

SUSAN'S CAMPING
At Appalachian State we used to rent a huge tent from the school and go camping with the girls from my Bible study and girls from the studies they were leading. We'd go to a state park near school and have a great time out in the mountains. It was amazing how much they liked this and how often we did it. It created unity and was a blast.

Common Concerns & Frustrations
You may find that you don't have a lot in common with some members of your group. Sometimes there isn't a natural affinity or even the desire to make friends with some in the group. Usually you'll be drawn toward some in your group more than others. This is normal. Take opportunities to let everyone

know you care about them and don't feel guilty about not being best friends with everyone in your group.

Another common frustration is time limitations. How do you find time to pursue your own friendships and still make friends with everyone in the group? One answer to this dilemma is to try to do activities with those in your group that you do anyway. For example, eating, going to class, doing laundry, attending Campus Crusade events, etc. See the following page for more ideas. Try some of these suggestions or come up with your own activities to get to know each other and build memories together.

50 Ways to Build Relationships

- Give them a call just to talk.
- Kidnap them for a coke, ice cream, shoot some hoops or take a walk when you know they are in the midst of heavy studying.
- Drop by with some cookies.
- Do laundry together.
- Go to church.
- Grab lunch or dinner together.
- Drop by for a brief, unscheduled visit.
- Go shopping.
- Walk to class.
- Play sports.
- Go to an athletic event.
- Go to a Campus Crusade function.
- E-mail them to tell them you're praying for a test they are having or a concern they have shared.
- Play a not too brutal practical joke on them.
- Drop by their room before their 8 a.m. class, bearing orange juice and a doughnut and walk with them to class.
- Run errands.
- Share Christ with someone.
- Ask for their help on anything:studies, a ride, advice, etc.
- Wash cars.
- Exercise.
- Have dinner at your place.
- Ask them if there is anything you could pray about for them.
- Make a midnight doughnut / coffee run.
- Go to a movie.
- Attend a concert.
- Go to a coffee shop between classes.
- Rent a video.
- Go on a summer project.
- Do something special for another person in the group.
- Join the same club.
- Go to a park and go hiking.
- Study together.
- Take some classes.
- Play on the same intramural team.
- Ride to a conference.
- Room together at a conference.
- Cook something.
- Go on a double date.
- Take them to your hometown.
- IM with them.
- Call them during school breaks, like Christmas, summer, etc.
- Have a video marathon with trilogies— like Star Wars, Anne of Green Gables or Lord of the Rings.
- Take a bike trip.
- Lay out in the sun.
- Go camping.
- Work on a project.
- Make a video.
- Pizza & studying.
- Watch a favorite TV show.
- Do volunteer work.

91

Activities to Do Together As A Group

- Go to an athletic event.
- Go shopping.
- Go to a movie.
- Attend church.
- Play sports together or challenge another group.
- Go to a lake, the mountains, or to an amusement park.
- Go to dinner out-of-town.
- Do an outreach together.
- Plan a creative date.
- Volunteer for Habitat for Humanity or Big Sisters/Big Brothers as a group.
- Spend the night at a group member's home.
- Have a car wash to raise money.
- Have a progressive dinner.
- Go on a road trip.
- Go to a group member's hometown.
- Go on a scavenger hunt.

Creative Group Dates

- Dessert in the park, or on top of the parking garage, or anywhere.
- Scavenger hunt with tape recorder, video camera, or Polaroid.
- Dinner on the quad.
- Go on a picnic.
- Make a video.
- Dinner on the beach—"The Sands" restaurant.
- Game night.
- Classic movie night.
- Progressive dessert.
- Kidnap someone.

How to Kill the Relationships in Your Group

- Send portions of their personal journal to the school newspaper.
- Punch them out when they foul you while playing basketball.
- Date their boyfriend or girlfriend.
- Have fun with your friends, but be serious with your group.
- This is important: never call them except to transmit information.
- Criticize their music, clothes, dorm room, major, family, hometown, girlfriend or boyfriend, weight, hair color or size of nose.

7.4

JESUS, PAUL & THEIR "SMALL GROUPS"

Jesus had a great set-up for His small group: He traveled, ate, slept, and spent hours teaching and ministering with them. There were structured times, like on the Mount (Matthew 5) when He taught them in a sermon, but many other important lessons were learned in settings outside of a formal teaching situation. Jesus shared His life with the twelve.

Paul wrote this to whom he ministered, "We loved you so much that we were delighted to share with you not only the gospel of God, but our lives as well" (1 Thessalonians 2:8).

We don't have the luxury of spending the kind of time Jesus or Paul spent with their small groups, but we can follow their lead of not only sharing God's Word, but also sharing our lives as well. In order to do this, we must develop relationships with our group members outside the group context.

CONCLUSION

This chapter has said a lot about relationships. This shouldn't surprise you, since relationships are central to small groups. You can't separate content from relationships. Christ brought the truth of the gospel, and He modeled a selfless love and concern for people. Likewise, God has given us both the message and ministry of reconciliation (2 Corinthians 5:11-21). Lives are transformed by the gospel in the context of relationships and it's crucial that group leaders understand how important relationships are to the process of "presenting everyone complete in Christ" (Colossians 1:28-29).

FOR THOUGHT / DISCUSSION

1 *Think of a group you've been in. How did the relationships in that group help your own walk with the Lord?*

   Read 1 Thessalonians 2:7-12.
   Answer questions 2, 3 and 4 using this passage.

2 *How would you describe Paul's heart toward those to whom he ministered?*

3 *Paul shared both the gospel of God and his own life with the Thessalonians. How can you also do both of these for your group?*

4 *What are some specific ways you can encourage, comfort and urge those in your group to live lives worthy of God? (1 Thessalonians 2:12)*

5 *Choose one or two group activities that might be fun for your group. Plan a time to make them happen. Choose some specific activities you can do with individuals in your group.*

94

BEVERLY'S FRIENDSHIP

One person who had a real impact on my life was my small group leader my senior year at the University of Texas. I hesitate to call her my small group leader because she was much more than that...she was a good friend. Lou Anne believed in me and gave me ministry opportunities most people thought I wouldn't be able to handle. Besides being involved in my life, she let me be involved in hers. Most of the year she was dating Steve, a guy at Rice University. One weekend we drove down to Houston together for a double date. My date was a guy in Steve's small group. Talking while traveling together really deepened our relationship. Lou Anne did more than just lead the small group I was in, she extended her life to me.

This chapter isn't a magic formula for building friendships, but suggestions of what's worked in the past. Maybe you'll have to take a different approach to building relationships or maybe God will have to do some miracles to bring your group together. Maybe it will never develop the sense

of community you desire. You can't control what will happen, but you can still take responsibility for initiating with those in your group. If they know you care about them, they will overlook your shortcomings. A group leader who honors God, cares about those in the group, and points others toward Christ has three of the most essential qualities in leadership.

95

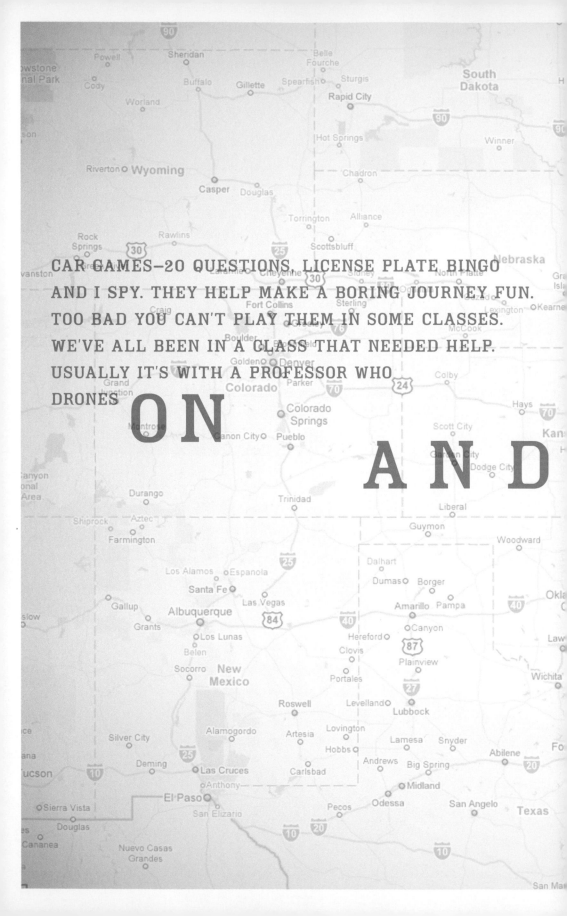

CAR GAMES—20 QUESTIONS, LICENSE PLATE BINGO
AND I SPY. THEY HELP MAKE A BORING JOURNEY FUN.
TOO BAD YOU CAN'T PLAY THEM IN SOME CLASSES.
WE'VE ALL BEEN IN A CLASS THAT NEEDED HELP.
USUALLY IT'S WITH A PROFESSOR WHO
DRONES ON AND

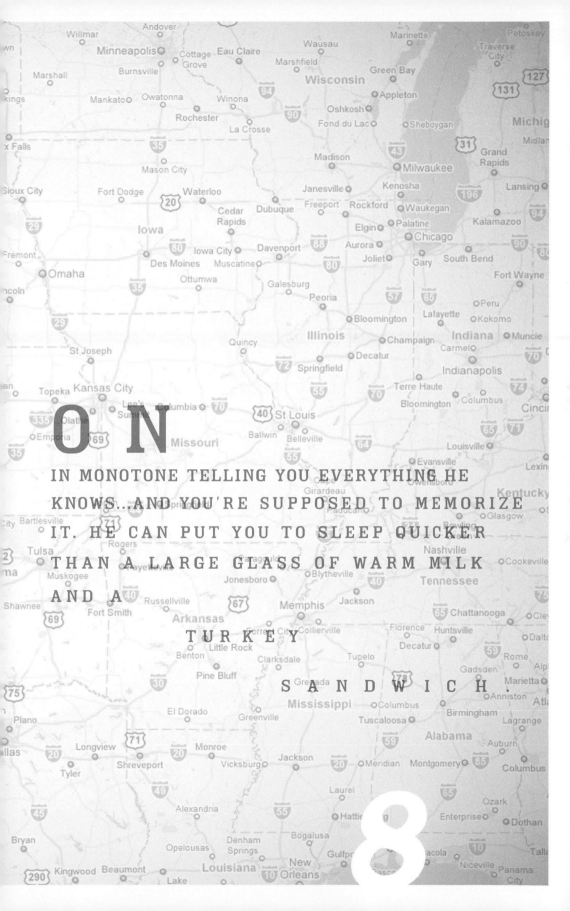

ON

IN MONOTONE TELLING YOU EVERYTHING HE
KNOWS...AND YOU'RE SUPPOSED TO MEMORIZE
IT. HE CAN PUT YOU TO SLEEP QUICKER
THAN A LARGE GLASS OF WARM MILK
AND A

TURKEY

SANDWICH.

8

20 QUESTIONS & OTHER CAR GAMES

Wouldn't you hate it if your group members dozed off like they do in boring classes? They won't if you lead your group right. Small groups have virtually nothing in common with a lecture. A successful group offers people the chance to learn for themselves, through interaction and mutual involvement. When this happens the experience is far from boring.

In this section you'll learn the art and science of asking good questions and using learning activities to stimulate your group to learn for themselves.

8.1

DIFFERENT TYPES OF QUESTIONS

Broadly speaking there are three types of questions—open, closed and limiting. It's important to understand each type of question, because there are a variety of ways you can use them in guiding your group.

Closed questions.
Closed questions are pointed and obvious. They imply the answer the leader

expects. An example would be, "Paul says we are to rejoice in everything, doesn't he?" Since they imply a "Yes" or "No" answer, there is little or no response from the group. Closed questions will inhibit group discussion and

ADVANTAGES OF ASKING QUESTIONS

- *Good questions make people think. When people think, they learn.*
- *Questions help you know whether the group is grasping the content. Without feedback you'll never know what your group is learning.*
- *Questions keep the group interesting.*
- *Questions cause group members to learn more together than they would have on their own.*
- *Questions enable the leader to focus and direct the discussion.*
- *Group interaction helps relationships develop within the group, which in turn helps learning and application.*

fail to promote self-discovered learning or community. When group leaders don't prepare they tend to naturally ask closed or limiting questions.

100

Limiting Questions.

Limiting questions limit the number of "correct" answers to a particular question. While closed questions should have no place in your small group, limiting questions can if they are used skillfully.

These questions cause the eyes of your group to look down to their Bible. For example, you may ask, "According to Ephesians 2:1-3, what does Paul say was true of every single one of us prior to coming to Christ?" The question is answered from the text and is not going to produce hearty discussion, but is necessary for uncovering the truth of the passage. And this discovery can lead to open-ended follow-up questions.

Open Questions.

Open questions don't imply an answer and are quite helpful for promoting discussion. They cause a person to think and, hopefully, learn. An example of an open question would be, "What do most students think about Jesus Christ?" or, "What do you observe in this passage? What seems important?" Open questions encourage group participation. The answers can be broad and varied. Open questions are more difficult to prepare, but they help make for a lively discussion.

8.2

GUIDING A DISCUSSION

Group discussion is like a captivating, well-played volleyball game. As the leader, you serve the ball by asking a good question. Then someone answers, setting up the ball for someone else in the group to respond, who then hits the ball to another individual. When the volley is dead, you serve up another question. The goal is not simply to keep the discussion going, but to direct it in such a way as to facilitate learning and life-change.

It takes practice, preparation and hard work to play an exciting game of volleyball, and the same is true in making good group discussion work.

There are a variety of ways to use questions. For example, if you were summarizing a lesson, it might be appropriate to use a limiting question such as, "How would you summarize the main emphasis of this passage?" However, at the beginning of a lesson you would want a wide open question

POP QUIZ

What types of questions are these? How would you respond?

- *John the Baptist baptized people, didn't he?*
- *Why do you think many students struggle in their Christian life?*
- *Are we saved by grace through faith or works?*
- *In 1 Corinthians 15:3-6, Paul says Jesus rose from the dead and appeared to Peter, then to the twelve, then to 500 of the brothers, then to James, then to all the apostles, and last of all to whom?*
- *You're never going to please God without confessing your sins, right?*
- *How would you describe the attitude on campus toward homosexuals?*

such as, "Would you consider yourself a patient person? Why?" Note that although the first part of the question is limiting, it sets up the wide open question which asks people to share about their struggles with being patient. Here are some helpful ways to use questions:

Launching Questions

A good way to start a study is using a wide open question that raises an is-sue that your passage will address. This is not just a "get to know you" kind of question, but one that links to your passage and possibly touches on an aspect of our Fallen Condition that's surfaced in the passage. For example:

- Describe a time in your life when you felt like you just couldn't measure up? (A possible lead-in question to a study on grace or forgiveness.)

- Name a hero you had growing up. What made you want to be like him/her? (This could launch a study on, say, Ephesians 5 where Paul exhorts his readers to "imitate God" or a 1 Timothy 4 study on "setting an example.")

Exploring Questions

After your launch question(s) and a brief summary of the passage, you will want to ask questions that help your group discover what God said. In order to arrive at the meaning of the passage, these questions should be both limit-ing and open-ended and should focus on the following:

What does it say? (observation questions)

- Ephesians 2:1-10, how does Paul describe the contrast between who they are now in Christ with who they once were?

- In Ephesians 2:4-7, what are the present realities of a believer's relationship with God?

What does it mean? (interpretation questions)

- In Ephesians 2:2, what does it mean that we once walked according to the ways of the world?

- In Ephesians 2:5, what does it mean to be made alive with Christ? (In order to get at Paul's meaning it would be helpful for your group to see the contrast between being "alive" and "dead in sin".)

What does it matter? (significance questions)

- In light of Ephesians 2:1-3, what would the rest of your life look like if God hadn't rescued you from your sin?

Before you move on to responding to Christ in application, you will want to help your group discover the big idea of the passage. Ask a question that helps them see the central theme or main point of the passage. For example:

• In Ephesians 2:1-10, what do you think Paul really wanted these believers to understand about grace?

Heart-level Response Questions

Your teaching will be most effective when it helps expose our Fallen Condition (a heart inclined toward finding life outside of a relationship with Christ) and when it points to Christ for the redemptive solution (chapter 5). Remember, you are not aiming at surface behavior, but rather, heart-level inclinations and motivations.

First, ask a couple questions that help them envision what it would look like to practically live out this passage. For example:

• In Ephesians 2:10, we are said to be Christ's workmanship. What should that look like in the life of a believer?

Next, ask a couple questions that expose heart-resistance to Christ. In other words, what is it in our Fallen Condition that is exposed in this passage? For example:

103

• Our culture tells us that we can become anything we want to become. How does this mindset subtly creep into your walk with God?

Next, ask a couple questions that point your group to Christ. What aspect of Christ's redemptive work do they need to believe and embrace in order to experience His grace and healing? For example:

• We often seek to control our future; why do we struggle with entrusting this to Christ? How would your life be different if you truly believed Jesus had only your best interest and greatest good in mind?

What you are attempting to do through these questions is to point them away from their natural proclivity to work harder at changing their behavior, and point them to Christ as the only source of growth and life. You can point them to Christ for forgiveness; you can point them to Christ for his empowerment to live the Christian life; you can point them to Christ to find hope in His promises; however you do it, point them to Christ.

Community and Conversation Questions

These are the questions that uncover the meaning of the text, the roots of our sin, and our response to Christ; these are the critical questions. That said, we don't want to undervalue all other types of questions you may ask.

As you ask heart-level questions, your Bible study should grow in authenticity, honesty, and community. But, it's also important to think through questions that are for the sole purpose of generating discussion and adding to the social dimension of the group. These are not insignificant. While your primary focus is for people to encounter Christ, you also need to make sure that they encounter one another, encountering Christ through community.

Becoming a Better Listener

Asking good questions is half the battle to having good discussion. Listening is the other half. When you listen as a leader, it shows you value the opinions and input of the group.

As you become a better listener, your questions become more pertinent and those in your group will more likely participate in the discussion. Here are some tips on how to accomplish this.

- Be an "in-their-shoes" listener, seeing the situation from their perspective. Try to understand the emotion expressed in their comments.

- Be an active listener. Your goal is to understand what the other person is communicating. If you are unclear about what they are trying to say, then rephrase in your own words what you believe was just said. This will give the other person a chance to correct you if you misunderstood the meaning. For example, "I'm not sure I caught that, Kristen. Let me see if I understand you. You think that Christians aren't lonely because they have a relationship with God. Is that right?"

- Be an encouraging listener. Many people need affirmation of their comments before they'll feel comfortable sharing anything more. Verbally respond to their questions and answers by saying something positive: "That answer shows you're thinking." "Great, that's right ..." (repeat what they said).

- Be a "total body" listener. Maintain eye contact with the person speaking and be aware of your posture. Certain positions (like crossing your arms or leaning back in your chair) communicate less concern than other positions, like leaning.

8.3

LEARNING ACTIVITIES

Good questions greatly aid self discovery, but there are other learning activities that further help you facilitate learning and application. These activities stimulate thinking and personal discovery and keep your group from being predictable. Try these out to add some variety and take your group to another level of learning.

1 Hypothetical Situation

Throw out a hypothetical situation for discussion related to the topic you are studying. This encourages group members to synthesize and apply what they're learning to a specific situation. For example:

105

- A friend comes to visit and you get into a discussion about Christianity. She comments, "I just can't buy Christianity because I don't see why Jesus is any more special than any other great religious leader." What would you say?

- Your boss asks you to lie to one of your customers or clients. What would you do?

- Your roommate who says he's a Christian didn't come home last night because he stayed at his girlfriend's apartment. What should you do, if anything?

2 Values & Culture

Tape a short section of a television show or movie (10-15 minutes maximum). Watch the clip and then discuss it from a biblical perspective. For example, you might examine how people make moral decisions, how they treat each other, what they value, what they think of Christianity, etc. You can do the same thing with popular songs, books, articles in the newspaper, etc.

3 Role Play

Act out a situation to identify with the characters. This is followed by a discussion of the scenario and the implications for the characters in the role play and to everyday life. The assignments for each of these roles are written out and given to individuals in advance. For example:

• Have your group members role play sharing the gospel with a friend.

• Take a story from the Bible and have different group members act out the parts. For example, use the story of the leper who came to Jesus (Mark 1:40-45). Assign them to read or assume different roles, i.e., the leper, Jesus, the disciples, the on-lookers. After the role play, ask the group how they felt about the leper, disciples, etc. Then ask them how they might have felt if they were the leper, or any of the other main characters. Ask who they identified with in the scene, and explore what it teaches about the character of Jesus and how they feel about Him.

4 *Debate*

Divide the group into two teams and assign an opposing view to each team. Give each team time to come up with the best evidence for their position. Set some rules for the debate and have fun. Then summarize the key points and their implications. For example:

• Did Jesus rise from the dead or is the resurrection simply a religious myth?

• Is the Bible God's Word, or a collection of religious stories that contain human errors?

• Is Christ a good moral teacher or God in the flesh?

• Is homosexuality a God-honored preference or a distortion of God's intent?

Obviously if you are going to use a debate format you must be prepared and clearly understand the issue.

In any small group things can and will go wrong. Here are three pieces of advice to help you. First, commit your group time to the Lord. Prepare your lesson and group time, trust Him with both, and then go have a good time. Second, learn to laugh at yourself. You'll make mistakes, so enjoy learning from them. Who has ever had a perfect group leader (besides the twelve disciples)? Third, love and care for those in your group. Caring goes a long way in making up for any mistakes you make.

A variation of the debate format is to divide the group in two and have a mock court room scene. One side represents the prosecution (opposing view) and the other side the defense. Have each side prepare a case and then have a trial. Possible topics are the resurrection, the reliability of the Bible, or the deity of Christ.

5 Brainstorming

The leader presents a problem to members of the group, who then come up with possible solutions. Offer suggestions in rapid succession. No comments, evaluations or criticisms are allowed at this time. After the list is completed and following a predetermined time allotment, the suggested solutions are discussed by the group, and biblical support (if not done so previously) is presented for each solution (if such support exists). For example:

* You have been studying evangelism and want to try a creative outreach to your non-Christian friends. Brainstorm an evangelistic event you might have ... a party, a dinner, a lecture series, etc. Let your imaginations go wild. Brainstorm all you would need to do to pull it off, including jobs people would need to do.

6 Demonstration

Bring in a couple of outside people to demonstrate how to perform a certain task. Afterwards discuss what happened and allow the group members to ask questions and analyze what they saw. For example:

* Working through a disagreement with a friend or relative.

* Sharing the gospel with a friend.

7 Research and Report

Present a question, problem or issue to the group relating to the topic of study. Ask group members to look into it and report back next week. For example:

* Read the school newspaper and/or a news magazine and bring back any stories, articles, or comments that relate to a particular issue, such as love, sex, forgiveness, lying, etc.

* Give them some passages to examine over the week and have them report back on what the Bible says about a topic, such as premarital sex or self-control.

* Let them read a chapter from a book you suggest and report on it. For example, a chapter on the resurrection from *Evidence That Demands a Verdict* (Josh McDowell) or one on an attribute of God out of *Knowing God* (J.I. Packer).

8 Storyboarding

Similar to brainstorming, except a task is proposed for the group to accomplish and the suggestions for accomplishing it are recorded on sticky notes and placed in categories or in the order of performing the task. For example:

107

- Assign the group to write a talk on prayer. They must decide the purpose of the talk, the questions their audience might be asking about prayer, the various pieces of relevant available information, Bible verses to include, an outline, and interesting anecdotes from the group members. The leader keeps the discussion lively.

CONCLUSION

Questions and learning activities are crucial to effectively capturing the interest of your group and creatively communicating God's Word. Don't fall prey to the ol' content dump method. Your group won't learn, and you won't be very encouraged in the process either.

Leading a group discussion is both an art and a science. There are skills you can learn and master, but each group session and group is unique. Once you learn the skills and gain experience, you will find that you become wiser and more comfortable as a leader.

108

FOR THOUGHT / DISCUSSION

1 *Writing good questions takes practice. Write two open questions which you might use to launch a lesson on:*
- *Pride (Romans 12:3).*

- *Obedience to the Lord (John 14:23-24).*

- *Wholesome talk (Ephesians 4:29).*

  Spend a few minutes familiarizing yourself with Philippians 2:1-11 in order to answer the following:

2 *From this passage, write an observation question that would help your group "see" what is in the passage.*

3 *Now, write an interpretation question that would help your group discover what a portion of this passage means.*

4 *Help them discover the significance of this passage by asking a question*

related to "What does it matter?"

5 *In the final step of helping your group explore the passage, write a question that would help uncover the big idea of this passage.*

6 *As you move into the response section, write a question that would help the group envision what it would look like to live out this passage.*

7 *Next, as you consider your own heart resistance to this passage, ask a question that would help uncover the group's Fallen Condition: the heart sin beneath the surface sin.*

8 *Finally, ask a question that would point to Christ as the solution to our heart resistance.*

How to Kill Self-Discovery

- Ask "Yes" or "No" questions. For example, "Is God's love like human love?" (These are 100% guaranteed discussion killers.)
- Ask leading questions when you should be using open questions, like this: "We struggle in our Christian life because we don't understand forgiveness, don't you think?" (Consider silence the norm if you ask this question.)
- Ask two-part questions that have "and" or "but" in them. Compound questions can be confusing. For example, "What does Paul say here and do you agree and how can you apply this principle?" (Questions like this are destined for blank stares.)
- Immediately answer your own questions. The leader asks, "How are we filled by the Spirit?" and before the group can think about it he answers, "Of course, by faith." (Group members aren't really even necessary if the leader hogs all the answers.)
- Fear silence and immediately fill it with some comment or answer. (Try some duct tape or a pair of rolled up socks if you can't help yourself from saying something.)
- Laugh or criticize a given answer. (This will do wonders for group participation and unity. Do it often enough and the last laugh will be on you.)
- Act like you know it all. (Your group members might not want to say much, fearing they'll sound stupid before their omniscient, all-wise leader.)
- Ask only objective questions, such as "What does the word 'believe' mean?" (Some of the most powerful questions relate to feelings. For example, "How do you feel when you slam the car door on your hand?")
- Ask questions regarding content only, and not application. (The goal is knowledge that leads to a changed life, not knowledge that leads to more knowledge. To get a little philosophical, Thomas Huxley once said, "The great end of life is not knowledge but action.")
- Wing it. Don't prepare questions ahead of time. Just go with the flow. (Good questions take time to prepare even if you are the King of Wing or Princess of Impromptu.)

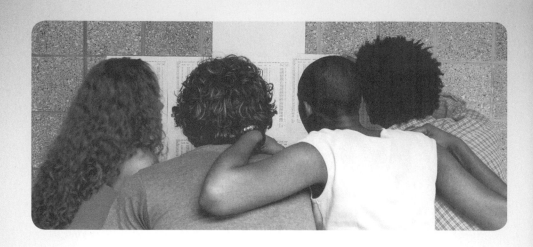

THREE TYPES OF QUESTIONS

TYPE	EXAMPLE	USE
OPEN Questions that allow group members to share any answer or relevant thoughts they may have on the subject or passage being studied.	"What truths stand out to you in this passage?"	Very valuable for group discussion. This kind of question stimulates thought and discussion, because there are no right or wrong answers.
CLOSED Questions that are obvious or imply the answer expected by the leader.	"Paul says we are to rejoice in everything, doesn't he?"	Questions like this are not valuable for discussion and actually stifle group interaction.
LIMITING Questions which limit the number of "correct" answers to a particular question.	"What three motivations does Paul mention in this passage?"	These questions aren't very valuable for open discussion, but they are necessary for helping to explore what the passage says and what it means..

SIX TYPES OF QUESTIONS

TYPE	EXAMPLE	USE
LAUNCHING	*"What's the most generous thing that someone has ever done for you?"*	*To cultivate interest in the study by raising an issue that your passage addresses.*
EXPLORING: OBSERVATION	*"In Ephesians 2:1-10, what kind of tone was Paul using to communicate?"*	*Questions that help answer, "What does it say?" to help the group discover what the author wanted to communicate to his readers.*
EXPLORING: INTERPRETATION	*"In Ephesians 2:1, what does it mean to be dead?"*	*Questions that help answer, "What does it mean?" in order to understand the original meaning of the passage.*
EXPLORING: SIGNIFICANCE	*"In light of Ephesians 2:4-10, why is it important to know that you are now and forever an object of God's love?"*	*Explores the question, "What does it matter?" to help the group see the significance of this passage in their life.*
EXPLORING: SUMMARY	*"In Ephesians 2:1-10, what is it that Paul really wanted his readers to understand about the God's love?"*	*Asks questions that help group members discover the big idea of the passage.*
RESPONSE	*"Twice in Ephesians 2:5-10, Paul emphasized that salvation is by grace and not by works. In what ways do you find yourself still trying to perform for God?"*	*Asks heart-level questions that expose our Fallen Condition and point to Christ as the solution.*

LIKE ANY ROAD TRIP, EVERY SMALL GROUP HAS ITS SHARE OF UNEXPECTED PROBLEMS AND DETOURS. THERE IS THE KILLER QUESTION: "WHAT'S THE RELATIONSHIP BETWEEN HUMAN WILL AND GOD'S SOVEREIGNTY?" OR YOU MIGHT EXPERIENCE THAT ONE GUY WHO WON'T STOP TALKING, WHO YOU KNOW HAS TO COME UP FOR AIR SOON (BUT NOT SOON ENOUGH FOR YOU). OR MAYBE SOMEONE MAKES

A HERETICAL STATEMENT, "THE BIBLE ISN'T AGAINST PREMARITAL SEX IF YOU LOVE THE PERSON." AND EVEN STRANGER *THINGS HAVE HAPPENED. WHO WOULD HAVE EVER THOUGHT PHILLIP WOULD START GIVING THE DETAILS OF HIS MOTHER'S AFFAIR, OR THAT DAWN WOULD BRING UP THE UFO SHE THOUGHT SHE SAW LAST SPRING, OR THAT KELLY WOULD EVEN CARE WHETHER HAIR GROWS IN HEAVEN?*

9

MANEUVERING THE POTHOLES

The crash of a small group discussion can be ugly. You may wonder what made you choose to lead a group. Leaders often struggle with the unexpected because they don't anticipate difficult situations and are unsure how to respond when they arise. You need to prepare for certain surprises. This chapter will examine some of the most common problems which come up in small groups. You've probably encountered most of them before, or if you haven't, you likely will in the near future.

9.1

TOP TEN DISCUSSION PROBLEMS

1 *Dead Silence*

"My group is totally silent after I ask a question. It's as if these guys have taken a vow of silence."

- If the question was good, relax; people need time to think. After some practice and getting to know your group, you'll find it easier to detect whether they're silent because they're thinking or because the question is a bomb. If you can't tell, ask, "Does what I'm asking make sense?"

- If the question wasn't good or just seemed to miss the point, ask one of the backup questions you've prepared to rephrase the question. For example, you asked, "Who do you have trouble forgiving?" and the group is silent. You aren't sure whether they are thinking about it, or scared, or didn't understand the question. You could ask a backup question such as, "Is there anyone you hold a grudge against? Would anyone like to share an example?" Remember to use open questions (see Chapter 8). Closed or limiting questions will silence anyone.

- Whatever you do, don't fill the silence with preaching. Feel free to contribute, but keep your own answers to a minimum and work on asking good questions.

- Choose learning activities directed toward their needs (see Chapter 8). Are you studying something that interests them? Are you presenting material which intersects with their lives?

- Encourage them with your nonverbal communication. Maintain good eye contact. Smile. Be relaxed. Lean toward the person speaking as you listen. Nod your head as you listen.

- Encourage them with your verbal feedback: Acknowledge and affirm each speaker with a non-judgmental response such as, "Thanks for your input." Compliment appropriate answers with responses like, "Excellent insight" or "Good thinking." Convey acceptance. Don't judge. Express appreciation when people grasp new ideas, express feelings or ask questions.

- Call on individuals who look like they have something to say.

2 A Wrong Answer

"The biggest problem I have is when someone gives the wrong answer. I just kind of sit there with a nervous smile and go, 'Uh ... Err ... Umm.'"

- Use discernment. Determine if it's a wrong answer or just a perspective different from yours.

- Be gracious and gentle. Don't get flustered.

- Redirect the question to another individual or to the rest of the group. Say something like, "Does anyone else have a different perspective or anything to add?"

- Refer the group back to the passage and use questions to guide them to discover the truths in it.

- If it's an off-the-wall response, say something like, "That's an interesting thought. How did you come to that conclusion?" Lead them to the truth gently.

  Note: At times it may be necessary to briefly give the correct answer if the group is unable to: "I can understand why you might think that, but..." For example, if someone strongly asserts the Bible is full of errors you can't simply move on to the next question.

- Use wisdom in determining which errors to handle in a group setting. It's best to avoid certain discussions in the group. For example, an erroneous comment such as, "God helps those who help themselves," can likely be corrected by the group. Furthermore, discussing this misconception is likely to be good for everyone in the group.

  However, be wary of a comment like, "The Bible doesn't prohibit homosexuality. In fact, most scholars think David was a homosexual." A possible response might be: "What passages have you read in the Bible about homosexuality? (Expect silence.) I don't want to chase that topic now, but I think if you read the passages for yourself you might conclude differently. I've got some information I can get to you." Then meet with the person individually.

- Exclude the inappropriate answers when you are summarizing.

3 Disastrous Distractions

"Every week in the middle of group some distraction always comes up. Usually the phone rings, someone comes in for a book, or everybody wants to leave early for a TV show."

- Ask whoever lives in the room if they can let their answering machine get the phone, or if they would be willing to unplug it.

- If all else fails, meet somewhere that's less distracting.

- If the group continually has schedule conflicts, re-evaluate the group time. For instance, if all freshmen have calculus tests every Tuesday, Monday night is

117

probably not the best time for a freshmen group.

CAUTION: If you need to permanently move your group time, do so. But don't begin to move it every other week because someone has something come up. Soon no one will know what time to come, and everyone will feel like group should be moved for them.

- Whatever the interruption, don't lose your patience. If you get exasperated or angry, you'll cause uneasiness in your group and only make it worse.

- If necessary, put a sign on the door. Be creative and not dogmatic. For instance, "BIBLE STUDY...KEEP OUT" is not what you want to communicate. Something like, "Bible study going on 7-8 p.m. Feel free to join us," might work better.

4 The Difficult Question

"The other day one of the guys asked me if Christ was going to come before the tribulation. I've read Revelation, but I'm not a Bible scholar."

- Admit you don't have a good answer, but tell them you'll look into it. Then ask someone older in the Lord, like your pastor or a staff member, if they know the answer or have the resources for you to study this yourself.

- Ask them why or what they want to know. It may be something they're only slightly curious about. You don't want to put hours of work into finding an answer someone is not really interested in knowing.

- It could be a great question for them to research and bring back to the group. They will learn more if they do the study themselves. You might need to give them some materials to get started.

5 Can't Finish the Lesson

"All the women in my group have such a good time together that I can't get through a lesson." This might happen for a couple of reasons. One, the members of your group like to talk, share, and joke around and it's hard for you to even get to the study, or two, the members of your group have so much to say about each question that you can't get through them all.

- If the basic problem is that they like to talk and share too much at the beginning of the group: Set some guidelines from the very start. Let them know

JERRY LOSES IT

One of the men in my group, Jerry, was a competitive, feisty character. He was leading his first freshman group in a lesson on how to be filled with the Spirit. About the middle of the lesson some non-Christian friends started rolling a manhole cover around on the concrete slab outside the room where the Bible study was meeting. It made a deafening roar, interrupting the group just like his friends planned. Jerry wasn't amused. The noise continued and Jerry lost it. He stormed out of the room and threatened to beat up the guys who were doing it. Then he coolly returned to leading his lesson on the Spirit-filled life.

CHIP'S DILEMMA

I was in a group with an emotionally wounded guy who dominated prayer, even to the extent that he prayed about things others had already prayed for. He prayed so long that others would open their eyes and look at each other, not knowing what to do.

there will be sometimes you'll just get together to share, play, and get to know each other. But the central purpose for your weekly time together is to spend time learning from God and His Word. So if they get carried away talking you can say, "OK, it's time to get back to learning from God and His Word, so let's get into the study."

Be careful with icebreakers. Keep them moving and don't let them eat up a lot of time, unless you've already allocated a large block of time for one.

- If the basic problem is spending too long on each question: Try to pace yourself. Prioritize your lesson. Allot a specific amount of time to spend on each section. For example, you might spend ten minutes on your introduction, twenty-five minutes in the biblical passage, and ten minutes discussing application. This will help you know when to move on. Don't be afraid to say, "This is all good, but we need to move on." Prioritize questions of greater importance and spend more time on those. Note which ones you'll omit if you are short on time. Encourage brief answers so more people will have time to speak.

NOTE: Some discussions are so profitable you won't want to move on. When that happens, be flexible. Choose an appropriate place to end the lesson on time. Next week you may want to pick up where you left off or move on to a new lesson.

119

6 The Non-Stop Talker

"I really like Dan, but he just talks and talks and talks. The other guys try to say something, and Dan interrupts them. Or it's like a ping pong match—they say something; then he says something. He dominates the group. Just once I'd like to see the other guys talk without a return volley."

- Direct your questions to other members in the group: "Let's hear from some of you who haven't had a chance to say anything yet."

- Sit next to the person and minimize eye contact.

- If it's still a problem, ask for the talker's help in drawing out quiet members or privately ask him to keep his answers to a minimum. No one wants to initiate this conversation, but if you let a bad situation go unchecked, it will hurt everyone in the group.

7 The Silent Member

"Whenever I'm with Tracy alone she's a chatterbox, but get her in a group, and it's hard to get her to say a thing."

- Ask direct but low-risk questions a shy person could answer comfortably. For example, "Tracy, I'd be interested in your thoughts. What are your thoughts on what we've been talking about?"

- Sit where you can maintain good eye contact with those who seem reluctant to speak out.

- Give positive feedback when the shy person does respond to encourage further responsiveness.

8 Going Off On Tangents

"I don't know how the guys did it but we started off talking about prayer, and before long we were talking about what sports we played in high school. These guys seem to have the spiritual gift of tangents."

OK, you've looked through this whole chapter, and your problem isn't among them. Maybe someone always shows up late, or people just don't show up at all no matter how many times you remind them. Or after several weeks, you've reached a point where you don't seem to be progressing. When you don't know what to do, pray. Ask God to give you wisdom and bind your group together in love. Pray also that He would create a hunger in them to continue to grow. This might be a good time to get some feedback from those in your group. And of course, you can also talk to your staff member or discipler about what to do. There's a sample evaluation you can use to get feedback from group members in the appendix. Whatever happens, don't get too stressed. Every great group has had its share of discussion disasters.

- Try to be diplomatic and reflect an accepting attitude.

- Use a good question to put the discussion back on the right track.

- Say something like, "That's an interesting topic, but since today we're focusing on _____, let's talk about that. If we have time later we can come back to this topic." As you gain experience, you'll learn when it's time to try to bring a group back to the subject.

- Jokingly say, "Well, speaking of our identity in Christ..." when the tangent is far removed from the actual topic.

9 Disagreements & Conflict

"These two women can't agree on anything, whether it's about guys or which of the Gospels tells the most complete story of Jesus. They're going to kill each other by the end of the semester."

- Don't let disagreements rattle you. Often they can aid in learning.

- If two people disagree on a certain point, it may be profitable to talk about the two opinions. It makes group members think and encourages interaction. Say something like, "This is good. It means both of you are thinking. Let's look at both of your ideas and see if we can sort out what the Bible says."

CAUTION: Whether it's appropriate to discuss a disagreement depends upon the subject. For example, if two people start arguing over the platform of the Republican Party, you wouldn't want to delve into either opinion because it won't help your study of God's Word. On the other hand, if two people are disagreeing whether James 2 and Romans 3 contradict each other, you could pursue both sides for the group's advantage.

If a disagreement persists that you don't want to address in group, say something like, "You guys might want to carry on that discussion after Bible study. Let's look now at the focus of our study today."

- If a disagreement is a matter of personal preference, sometimes it's best just to move on. You can say something like, "I suppose we all have our opinions on that," and continue the lesson.

- If two group members regularly bicker, you might need to talk about it with each of them. Remember, problems won't just go away.

10 Leader Answering All the Questions

"My group members are always asking me what I think. Then I end up telling them, and I feel like I do all the talking."

Rather than tell them the answer, help them discover it for themselves. Use questions to help them get their focus back on the issue. Here are some ways you can respond when someone asks you a question you want them to answer:

- Direct another question to a specific person in the group. "Judy, what are some things Paul says about love in this passage?"

- Reverse the question back to the person who asked it, "That's a good question, Steve. What do you think?"

- Relay the question back to the whole group, "That's a good question. What do you all think?"

CONCLUSION

You can eliminate most small group discussion crashes by planning and preparing well. Work hard at knowing your group members' needs. This will ensure your discussions are relevant and will help you know how to respond.

Learn the art of asking good questions and using learning activities to involve the entire group. Learn to trust the Lord with your efforts. A good sense of humor will usually help—something just about always seems to come up. Over time you'll be able to tell some great stories of things that happened in groups you led.

FOR THOUGHT / DISCUSSION

1 What is your greatest fear concerning what might happen when you are leading a group? Go ahead, say it. What is a good way to deal with this if it occurs?

2 How would you deal with the following situations:

- You've just asked a question you thought was brilliant, but now you realize it wasn't even understandable. Blank stares greet you everywhere you look.

- One of the men in your group says he wants to watch a Final Four basketball game during group next week. Everyone else seems to agree.

- Someone in your group has just begun to vigorously assert that if you don't believe in a "young earth" theory of creation you aren't a Christian. Everyone is on edge.

- You're leading a lesson on forgiveness and one of the women in the group starts crying.

123

How to Discourage Your Group Members
"Hey, Judy, are you fanning yourself, or have you still not found 1 Corinthians?"
"Good, Troy. That would have been the right answer if I'd asked a different question.
"I like your Bible, Candy. I didn't know they made a Precious Moments' Bible."
"Larry, how did you come up with so much to say this week? I thought you'd be worn out from last week."

IT'S FRIDAY NIGHT. YOU'RE ON YOUR WAY TO VISIT YOUR GIRLFRIEND AT BERKELEY. IT'S ONLY A COUPLE HOURS DRIVE, BUT IT'S GETTING LATE BECAUSE YOU DIDN'T GET OFF WORK UNTIL 8:00. THIS FRIDAY IS DIFFERENT THAN MOST—IT'S YOUR ONE YEAR ANNIVERSARY OF DATING, YOU PLANNED DINNER AT AN EXPENSIVE RESTAURANT, BUT NOW YOU COULD BE FACING AN UPSET GIRLFRIEND. JUST THE THOUGHT OF BEING

LATE MAKES YOU DRIVE A LITTLE FASTER. AROUND THE BEND IN THE INTERSTATE YOUR HEADLIGHTS PICK UP A BROKEN DOWN CAR ALONG THE SIDE OF THE ROAD. A YOUNG WOMAN STARES AT THE STEAM POURING OUT OF THE OPEN HOOD, WHILE TWO KIDS ARE PERCHED ON THE TRUNK. AT FIRST YOU THINK YOU MIGHT STOP AND HELP, BUT THEN YOU REMEMBER YOUR DATE. YOU EASE OVER INTO THE FAR LANE, STARING INTENTLY AT THE ROAD AHEAD, *AND SOON THEY FADE FROM SIGHT IN YOUR REAR VIEW MIRROR.*

10

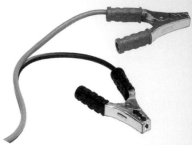

CHAPTER 10

HELPING STRANDED MOTORISTS

Jesus told a similar story about people who were too preoccupied, cal-loused or scared to help others. We know the story as the parable of the Good Samaritan (Luke 10:25-37). In this story a foreigner goes out of his way to help a total stranger. Jesus didn't tell His parable as a reminder to travel safely, carry a cell phone, and join AAA. Rather, He told it to illustrate the care we should have for other people. It ends with these words, "Go and do likewise" (Luke 10:37).

Many small groups study the Word and provide strength and encourage-ment for the members to walk with God. This is how it should be. But sadly, often groups never turn the corner from "getting" to "giving." They never exist for anything beyond the group itself. This isn't how it's supposed to be.

You can't separate loving God from loving and caring for people. When an expert in the law asked Jesus which is the greatest commandment in the Law He replied, "'Love the Lord your God with all your heart and with all your soul and with all your mind.' This is the first and greatest commandment. And the second is like it: 'Love your neighbor as yourself.' All the Law and Proph-ets hang on these two commandments" (Matthew 22:37-40).

Jesus' answer is stunning. The most important issue in life is relationships—our relationship with God and relationships with other people. The Christian life is both a passion for our God and Savior, and a passion for those for whom He came. As we grow in our love for God, we'll love what He loves—people. If you love God, you love people.

So, all small groups should ultimately be committed to both of these priorities. Each group will go about pursuing these commandments in different ways, depending upon the purpose and maturity of the group.

10.1

MOVING FROM GETTING TO GIVING

It's important for leaders to be committed to helping those in their group learn to care for and be involved in the lives of those outside the group. This doesn't imply that those in the group cease getting and only give. During our entire Christian lives we're getting from God and from other believers. Ideally, believers in a small group should receive, and then give.

Learning to turn the corner from getting to giving is often a difficult step for many Christians, because it's far safer to stay within the confines of the group. However, someone cannot love God without caring about others;

128

JUDY'S TREAT

Lynne, one of the girls in my Bible study at Vanderbilt, was doing her student teaching at an inner-city school. That Halloween she invited some of her fourth graders to join us for trick-or-treating. Hand in hand we went from door to door with our new friends. The little girls loved the chance to feel safe and loved by some college students. After trick-or-treating we gathered at my house to check out the goodies. We told them about the most important thing in our lives—our relationships with Christ. I shared the gospel and eight of them trusted Christ. It was a fun experience for us and a life-changing one for them. What a treat.

"Dear friends, let us love one another, for love comes from God. Everyone who loves has been born of God and knows God. Whoever does not love does not know God, because God is love" (1 John 4:7-8). A good small group will reflect the priority of loving and caring for people.

When a group works together to give to others, there are many benefits. Other people have their needs met by hearing the Good News. Also, the group itself grows closer together, and its compassion for others deepens. Perhaps, greatest of all, they get more excited about Jesus.

How do you help your group get involved in giving? There are two key steps: first, help them see the needs of those around them. Second, give them opportunities to get involved in meeting some of these needs.

1   *Help them see.*

Jesus was motivated to care for others because He saw their needs. "When he saw the crowds, he had compassion on them, because they were harassed and helpless, like sheep without a shepherd" (Matthew 9:36). He saw needy individuals. And He was compassionately moved to help them.

Today it's often difficult for us to see the needs of others. Society fosters independence, isolation, and self-focus so most people are not aware of the needs of others. They are least aware of their spiritual needs.

Your group members must begin to see beyond themselves. Here are four ways to help a group begin to do this.

129

* First, help them develop biblical convictions about the needs of people. When group members view their family and friends through the values of society, they may not see their spiritual needs, so they lack any motivation to help. An attractive, successful, popular student who doesn't know Christ is rarely viewed as "harassed and helpless" and "lost" as the Bible describes this person.

Some Biblical Words
Used to describe those who don't know Christ.

* *Dead*
* *Disobedient*
* *Objects of wrath*
* *Harassed*
* *Helpless*
* *Godless*
* *Wicked*
* *Suppressers of the truth*
* *Darkened*
* *Fools*
* *Stubborn*

* *Unrepentant*
* *Self-seeking*
* *Followers of evil*
* *Rejecting the truth*
* *Perishing*
* *Without excuse*
* *Accountable*
* *Deceived*
* *Slaves to sin*
* *Cannot please God*
* *Destined for everlasting punishment*

GARY'S ROOFTOP
When I led a small group at the University of Tennessee, I would take each guy to the top of an academic building overlooking campus. Below us were thousands of students, going back and forth from classes. I would ask each of the guys, "How many of those students do you think know God personally?" It was a sobering statement but a great way to build compassion into the group. Then we would pray for the campus.

SUNG'S TOMBSTONE
My leader took our small group to a cemetery one day. We talked about what we would like written on our tombstone. We read names, dates, and inscriptions, and talked about life in general. It was a great wake-up call to the nature of life, the finality of death, and the importance of the gospel.

Your group will benefit by studying passages in the Bible describing the spiritual needs of those who don't know Christ. Romans 1:18-3:20 argues how they are rightfully guilty before God (3:9-10) because of their rejection of what God has made plain to them (1:18-20). They worship created things instead of the Creator (1:25) and have fallen short of the glory of God (3:23). Ephesians 2:1-3 describes the state of a person who doesn't know Christ. Revelation 20:11-15 and 2 Thessalonians 1:5-10 depict the tragic fate of those who ignore God's offer of forgiveness and reconciliation.

- Second, help your group develop a heart for others by studying passages which reveal God's heart for people. Pray that God will help you see as He sees and feel what He feels. Some passages which reveal God's heart for people are Matthew 9:35-38, Luke 15, Romans 5:6-8, Luke 13:31-34, Mark 1:40-45 and Luke 19:1-9.

- Third, expose your group to the needs of people. Use examples from everyday experiences, such as articles in the school paper, conversations, news events, etc. When you are in situations with group members, like going to class, McDonald's, or the cafeteria, seize the opportunity to talk about peoples' needs. Perhaps go off campus to see the needs of people, like to a soup kitchen, nursing home or AIDS hospice.

One way to expose your group to the spiritual needs of people is to take surveys around campus. Design questions that fit your particular audience. Have each person take as many surveys as possible and then compile a list of the top ten needs they see on campus. This will give them a glimpse into the hearts and minds of other students.

Some possible survey questions could include: •What are the greatest needs of people you know? •If you could have one thing you don't have right now, what would it be? •What do you think are the two greatest fears of our generation? •What do you think is the solution for the problems you see in the world? •If a young child asked you, "What happens when people die?," what would you say? •If you could have one question answered about life, what would you want to know?

- Fourth, hold a focus group. Ask ten or so non-Christians to get together for pizza to give you honest feedback on how they think and feel about Christianity. The goal of the time is not to answer their questions, but to honestly listen to what they are thinking and feeling. This may also lead to your group developing some relationships with non-Christians.

    Some possible Focus Group questions could include: •What do you perceive is the basic message of Christianity? •What do you like or dislike about Christianity? •How did you form these opinions? •What is your opinion of Christians at this school? •How many of your friends share your views? •If you were a Christian at this university, what would you do to improve your image?

2 Give them opportunities to meet needs.

One of the best ways to expose your group to needs around them is to give them opportunities to give to others. Remember to consider the maturity of your group when you plan an activity designed to help them turn the corner to giving. If you expect too much from a group too fast, they'll be reluctant to do anything.

MELVITA'S PILGRIMAGE

I wanted the women in my group to understand what we were studying in Romans 1 and 2. So, I took them on a religious pilgrimage around the city of Washington, D.C. After leaving Howard University, we went to a Hindu temple, a Mormon temple and an Islamic center. I wanted them to observe and learn about these different groups.

Afterwards, the girls came over to my place for dinner, discussion and to watch the "JESUS" film. We saw how people are lost and without excuse. We talked about the blindness of people and the task ahead for us to reach them.

It was good for the girls to have God open their eyes to the hopelessness of people and the possibilities of God.

As the leader set an example by sharing your own heart and convictions concerning reaching out to others. Even in a brand new group you can tell about a conversation you had with a friend about Christ. Just like many other

SHERRIE'S DATE WITH CHRISTIANS

I had a date to the spring formal, but I really wanted to get in with a group of people so it wouldn't be awkward. My roommates were involved in Campus Crusade, and a large group of them were going to dinner together. I asked if we could come along, even though I wasn't a Christian or involved in Campus Crusade. They welcomed us, and that night I had a blast. In fact, I had never had that much fun sober. Over the next few weeks I started attending the Campus Crusade meetings. My friends told me about God and eventually I became a Christian. My senior year I had the chance to lead my own group. It all started because of a fun social adventure with a group of Christians.

issues in life, compassion for others is often caught from others. Take individuals in the group with you while you do ministry and they will often come back personally motivated to do the same.

Even the youngest group can give to others with simple activities, such as eating dinner with a group of non-Christians, bringing cookies to someone who's discouraged, praying for someone, inviting a friend to an evangelistic event, tutoring a student who needs help, or help at a food drive or other project on campus. Activities like these aren't threatening to most young group members, but they still help build a caring attitude about those outside of the group.

10.2

THE ULTIMATE GIFT

A group can reach out to those around them in many ways, but none is more important than reaching out with the good news of the gospel. Because the greatest need any person has is to be reconciled to God, the ultimate gift we can offer someone is to introduce them to Christ.

Since its beginning in 1951, Campus Crusade for Christ has focused on meeting peoples' spiritual need. Dr. Bill Bright, founder and president of Campus Crusade, often asks these two questions: "What is the greatest thing that has ever happened to you? What is the greatest thing you can do for others?" These two questions reveal the heart and motivation behind a worldwide ministry committed to offering Christ to the world. Much has changed over the past decades, but our purpose remains the same: to glorify God by helping to fulfill the Great Commission.

The Great Commission was Jesus' final command to His disciples (Matthew 28:16-20). While Jesus was with them He taught getting and giving. They received from the Lord and went out into the towns and villages to give to others. Now, after His death, they received the ultimate gift, Jesus' death and resurrection on their behalf. They in turn passed it on, being faithful to help fulfill the Great Commission by making disciples throughout the world.

There are many ways for small groups within Campus Crusade to help fulfill the Great Commission. Not all groups are structured the same way, not all groups have the same purpose or content, and not all groups are directly focused on doing evangelism. However, every campus ministry within Campus Crusade has adopted the mission to help "turn lost students into Christ-centered laborers." In some form or fashion, each small group within Campus Crusade should help fulfill this mission.

133

Turning lost students into Christ-centered laborers is a process. Younger group leaders help individuals first develop a heart for those who don't know

JAY'S EXAMPLE

I'll never forget the first time my group leader, Jay, asked me if I wanted to come along when he talked to someone about Christ while we were at Daytona Beach, Fla. I was terrified, but he was quite calm, and before long he was sharing with this guy who was catching rays beside his car. The guy trusted Christ. I figured that was the end of a good day and it was time to hit the surf, but Jon just went on down to talk to another guy. I think God must have been out to encourage me as a rookie because that day all five guys Jon shared with received Christ. Going along with him changed me more than any lesson ever could have. Later that week I shared Christ for the first time.

Christ and help them begin to share Christ with others. Usually students need help doing this. They need to be with the group leader as he models how to share his faith. The group leader needs to give them training in how to share the gospel using the "Four Spiritual Laws" or "Would You Like to Know God Personally?".

Bad Ideas on Moving from "Getting" to "Giving"
- *Offer $5 for each person your group members share Christ with. If compassion doesn't motivate them, who knows...maybe money will.*
- *Surprise your group by suggesting they hit the quad for some outdoor preaching next Friday at noon. This will win them over to the joy of sharing Christ in a hostile environment.*
- *Ask a young group to start a new evangelical church in downtown Baghdad.*
- *Ask them to do something you aren't doing, like talking to unbelievers.*

As group members mature in Christ, they often desire to start their own small groups. When this happens, the veteran leader takes on a new role by equipping the younger believers in the group with skills they need to lead their own groups.

As lost students become Christ-centered laborers, more students become actively involved in giving the ultimate gift to others. God's great gift and His Great Commission are at the heart of all we do in Campus Crusade for Christ.

10.3

OTHER IDEAS FOR REACHING OUT

There are a variety of ways your group can reach out to others. It's up to the leader to choose the wisest course for the group in light of its maturity and purpose. Here are some ideas on different ways your group can give to others.

1 Have a "bring a friend" small group meeting where everyone invites a non-Christian to the group. In fact, some small groups are designed to be open groups, where members are encouraged to bring new people every week. Do a lesson or activity that would be appropriate for everyone. Cru.comm (see chapter 12) contains two evangelistic Bible study series.

2 Do something as a group to give to others, such as Habitat for Humanity, Special Olympics, or a leukemia drive. Sometimes taking students off campus deepens their heart to share Christ on campus.

3 Meet together regularly to pray.

4 Invite non-Christian friends along for some sort of adventure, such as paint ball, camping, attending a formal, or simply going out for pizza.

5 Plan a group outreach of some kind. You could do an evangelistic meeting in a dorm or fraternity/sorority or plan a party. Another option is handing out evangelistic articles to friends and getting their feedback on it or putting up flyers for the evangelistic website, EveryStudent.com. Maybe the group could show the "JESUS" film to international students.

6 Take a missions trip together.

CONCLUSION

Remember that a group will tend to become ingrown by focusing on its own needs. Being involved in ministering to others is essential to following Christ. A group that pursues loving God will naturally love and pursue people as a result.

135

ALYSIA'S VALENTINE

For a long time I had been feeling compassion for Debbie, who lived next to me, but I never seemed to be able to work up the nerve to just talk to her about Christ. Our small group decided to have a Valentine's Day party, so I invited Debbie. We had an icebreaker, food and door prizes. One of our women was the emcee, one led the icebreaker, one gave her testimony, and our small group leader gave a talk called "Keeping the Love Alive." After the offer to receive Christ, Debbie said, "Yes." On the drive back after the party, she said it was the first time she had ever heard the gospel explained.

JENNIFER'S TRIP

I participated in a life-changing inner-city missions project with Campus Crusade one summer. I was able to share my faith, make friends in the neighborhoods of New York, and help meet some physical needs around me. The next fall, we recruited a men's small group to go with our group to New York for spring break. Twelve of us flew up to New York together. We had the best time showing the "JESUS" film, sharing our faith, and helping meet the needs of the homeless.

FOR THOUGHT / DISCUSSION

1 *What helped you turn the corner from getting to giving in your Christian life? How would you say you are presently doing in this area?*

2 *In 2 Corinthians 5:16, Paul writes, "So from now on we regard no one from a worldly point of view." What are some ways you view people around you from a worldly point of view? What would you see in people if you didn't see them from a worldly point of view?*

3 *Have you ever been in a group that did some kind of ministry together? What did the group do? What was the result, both outside and inside of the group?*

4 *If someone told you they didn't think it was that important for a Bible study to be involved in giving to others, what would you say? How would you defend your view using God's Word?*

5 *Given the maturity level of your group and its purpose, what are some creative ways your group can reach out together?*

- -

EMPTY TANK ?

Turning a group from getting to giving is often difficult. Not everyone in the group will want to be involved in evangelism or the other ways of giving to others. Even if you do a good job leading the group in this direction, you'll likely encounter resistance. It's often threatening for group members to publicly associate with Christ. If this happens, remember God the Father cared enough about people to offer His Son, who was misunderstood, maligned and crucified. Being faithful to share Christ with others isn't easy, but it's better than the alternative of being too frightened to get involved with others.

137

IT'S EASY TO TAKE A WRONG TURN ON
A REAL ROAD TRIP.
ALL YOU NEED TO DO IS GET DISTRACTED TALKING TO A FRIEND
AND MISS A SIGN. WHAT A BUMMER TO DRIVE MILES OUT OF
YOUR WAY OR GO IN THE WRONG DIRECTION! IT'S ALSO QUITE EASY
TO GET OFF TRACK WITH A SMALL GROUP. DOWN THE ROAD YOU'LL
WANT TO EVALUATE TO SEE IF YOU'VE BEEN ON THE RIGHT ROAD.
AS YOU CREATIVELY EVALUATE YOUR SMALL GROUP, YOU'LL
BENEFIT YOURSELF AND YOUR GROUP MEMBERS AS YOU ADJUST
YOUR GROUP'S DIRECTION.

30,000 MILE CHECK-UP

You'll find it helpful to evaluate your group in two different ways. First, it's important to evaluate after each session. This will help you learn how to be a more effective leader. Second, regularly ask yourself if the group is making progress toward the objectives and purpose you set for it. This will help you keep the group headed in the right direction.

11.1

EVALUATING A GROUP SESSION

Evaluating a group session helps you identify what you did well and what needs improvement. Avoid the tendency to sell yourself short in your leadership skills:

"I did such a lousy job no one will come back next week." But don't go to the other extreme and think too highly of your skills: "That was the best small group these guys have ever been in. I did a great job." Evaluation will help you get an accurate picture of how you are doing as a leader.

It's important to get feedback and learn from it. No matter how much experience you have in leading a small group, spend a few minutes after each group meeting reflecting about your group time. You might find it helpful to think about these five areas:

1 Preparation.

Were you well prepared? Did you pray for the group time? Is there anything you wish you had done? Did you prepare good back-up questions? Did you work through the lesson for yourself? Did you share out of your own experience?

2 Session plan.

Did the different elements of the group (sharing, prayer, lesson, etc.) seem to be helpful for the group? Did one element run long? What can you do differently next time?

3 Group discussion.

Could any of your questions have been better? Did any situation arise that you wish you had dealt with differently, such as tangents or conflicts? What was the atmosphere during the study? Did members seem relaxed? What can you do to make people feel more comfortable?

4 Time in the Word.

Did the students get into the Word and profit from it? Were they able to derive a principle and come up with a personal application? What would help you more effectively communicate God's Word next time?

5 Other details.

What went on in the small group apart from the lesson? Who wasn't there? When did everyone show up? Is this still a good time to meet? Is this the best place to meet? Did we start on time? End on time? Were there any distractions?

Some of these may be tough questions to answer objectively. One way to gain objective input is to invite your group leader (or another experienced person) to visit your group. After the meeting, gather your leader's feedback.

If it isn't possible to have your leader sit in on the group time, you can still sit down together later and discuss what went on. Your leader will be able to ask you questions to lend perspective to you.

No matter how experienced you are at leading a group, there is always room for improvement. At the beginning, there may be a number of areas where you need to improve. That's OK. Pick one and work on it for next time.

Don't expect too much at once. You learn a new skill by breaking it into bite-sized pieces and working on one at a time. This guidebook lays out the various pieces of leading small groups so you can isolate and concentrate on one piece at a time. For example, if you want to work on learning activities and questions, see Chapter 8. If you got stuck knowing how to respond to a situation that came up in group, see Chapter 9.

NOTE: There is a sample evaluation in the appendix that you might find helpful to evaluate a group session.

11.2

MID-COURSE ADJUSTMENTS

143

Periodically you should stop to evaluate the progress your group is making toward your purpose and objectives. Sometimes leaders are so busy getting to know their group members and preparing for each lesson they fail to examine the direction they're going in. Mid-course evaluations are profitable because the leader now knows far more about her group than she knew at

> **HELPING ROOKIES**
> Whenever someone in my group first started leading a group I would try to sit in on the group for a few weeks. After each group I would tell him what he did well and ask him what he learned from leading that particular group. I'd also give him some ideas on things he might have done better. I learned a lot from watching those groups, and the new leaders really appreciated being coached along the way.

the beginning. It's usually not too late to make changes that will help you, and the group, better fulfill its purpose.

The first step in checking your progress is to get some feedback from your group members. This can be done verbally or through written form. If you're a first time group leader, using a simple tool after the first four or five weeks may be helpful. A good rule of thumb is to use a written evaluation no more than once per quarter or semester. A sample of a possible evaluation is included at the end of this chapter.

The second step in evaluating the progress of your group is to consult the "Purpose and Content" sheet you filled out in Chapter 4. If you didn't fill something like this out for your group, now's a good time to think about these issues.

As you look over the purpose and goals sheets, ask God for wisdom concerning any adjustments you can make to better meet the needs of those in the group.

For example, maybe after a few weeks you've seen needs that you weren't aware of when you first planned your group. After getting to know the group you might want to slightly alter the content. Remember the goal isn't to get through a set number of lessons but to help your group members take the next steps in their personal walks with God.

The third step in evaluating your group is to go back to the five crucial elements of a good small group discussed in Chapter 2. Look at how your group is doing in each area and consider what changes you might make to do better in each one. Remember that groups develop over time, so consider the purpose and maturity of your group when evaluating it.

How to Tell When Your Evaluation is Going Bad
* *One of the girls asks how to spell "incompetent."*
* *Your group members are writing on the back, along the side and asking for extra paper.*
* *They pull out their laptops to illustrate graphically how bad a leader you are—a picture is worth a thousand words.*
* *They ask, "Now, you're sure your group leader will see this?"*
* *One girl gets writer's cramps working on the question, "What can I do to improve the group?".*

1 Quality Biblical Content

Is the biblical content helpful to those in your group? Is it addressing their needs? Is the group learning to delve into God's Word?

2 Community

Is the group getting to know each other? Are they working together as friends and beginning to care about the well-being and spiritual growth of each other? Are they spending time together outside of the group? Are they beginning to feel ownership of the group ("our" group)?

3 Richly Experiencing Christ

Are group members growing in their knowledge and relationship with Christ? What can you do to help them to experience Christ?

4 Progressive Life-Change

Are those in your group applying what they are learning? Is application important to the group? (See Chapter 5.)

5 Outward Impact

145

Depending upon the maturity of your group, are they giving out to others? Are they beginning to change from getting to giving (Chapter 10) or is the group still inwardly focused? Are group members learning to share Christ with others?

Once you've evaluated how your group is moving toward its purpose and objectives, you can make some changes if needed. Perhaps you need to modify your content, change the different elements of the group (prayer, sharing, time in the Word, etc.), or plan some kind of group activity or outreach.

Each group is different, but the principle of mid-course evaluation is valid regardless of the group's maturity. You may be tempted to compare yourself with others or the evaluation process may be discouraging. Success isn't based on how your group measures up to someone else.

Remember, not only is your group in process, but you are too! It's better to see where you can improve than to pretend everything is great.

As you maintain a commitment to grow as a leader, you'll be greatly encouraged as you look back and see how much you've improved. Paul offers great encouragement, saying, "Therefore, my dear brothers, stand firm. Let nothing move you. Always give because you know that your lbor in the Lord is not in vain" (1 Corinthians 15:58).

Small Group Members' Evaluation

1 I look forward to coming to this small group: yes/no/sometimes. Why?

2 I benefit from this time: yes/no/sometimes. For example:

3 I wish we would do the following:

4 I feel a part of the discussion during the group time: Yes / No. Why?

5 Other comments or suggestions:

CAUTION: DEALING WITH DISAPPOINTMENT

Not everyone goes on to grow in their walk with the Lord in any given Bible study. This is quite disappointing to a young group leader. It should be. We should always be sad when anyone loses interest in the Lord or His Word. However, being disappointed is different from feeling responsible or being discouraged.

If God blesses you with many different groups in your lifetime, never grow tired of being sad when people make poor decisions. You can't control the outcome, but don't stop caring.

11.3

KNOWING WHEN TO CALL IT QUITS

There comes a time in all small groups to call it quits. This can come about for obvious reasons, such as summer break, graduation or nuclear explosion. Don't let a group drag on simply because it's easier to keep going than to change. Ending a group can often be in the best interest of everyone involved.

There are several reasons a leader might want to end a group. Some are more encouraging to the leader than others.

The first is that its purpose has been fulfilled. For example, maybe the group is an evangelistic group, and its purpose was to present the gospel from the Gospel of John over a few weeks. Or, perhaps the group was formed to study prayer and revival, and after eight weeks you think it's best to start a new group focused on evangelism.

A second reason to call it quits is if the group is a "cell group." Cell groups, by definition, are open to new members every week. When these groups get large, they multiply by splitting to form new groups.

A third and more disheartening reason to end a group could be waning enthusiasm or numbers. Despite a noble effort by a faithful group leader, a group still may not thrive. If there are only two (or less) people coming to the group maybe it's best to join with another group, or make some changes to pick up a few more people.

Sometimes group members lose interest in the Bible study. When a leader first notices this she should consider some of the options in the box "How to Add Vitality to a Boring Group." Often a group leader can do a great job, but people still might drift away.

147

Maybe you've reached the point where nothing seems to work. No matter what you do, those in your group seem content to stay where they are, no matter how much you pray or how many changes you make in the group.

Remember there is far more to spiritual growth than offering a good lesson in a good group. Individuals within the group must be willing to learn from

HOW TO ADD VITALITY TO A BORING GROUP

- Ask God for wisdom.

- Ask a staff member or veteran group leader to sit in on your group and give you help.

- Get honest feedback from group members about what they like/dislike. You can do this with a survey or through casual conversations.

- Reassess the needs of the group (Chapter 4). Are you connecting with their lives?

- Re-read Chapter 6 on asking questions and learning activities. What can you do to make the group more exciting and relevant?

- Look at Chapter 7 on relationships. Try doing a few things as a group outside of group time, or build relationships with individuals outside of the group.

God's Word and apply it to their lives. Every person can willfully be disinterested in the group, despite a good leader. Recognize that while you can be responsible to faithfully lead and pray for those in the group, you can't take the responsibility for everyone attending.

A fourth reason it might be time to call it quits is when the group becomes divided in terms of spiritual maturity. Over time some group members will want to get deeper into the Word and press on in their walks with the Lord. At the same time, there may be others who are struggling. When this happens both groups of people can be frustrated, feeling the lesson or group isn't helpful to them. If everyone wants to work at it, a group like this can still flourish. There may also be wisdom in starting two groups or reconsidering its direction.

Although it may seem like a failure at first, ending a group might be the best thing for you and those in your group. You may be able to find a better place for some, and others might realize they no longer want to be in any study. Maybe they will change their hearts and decide to follow Him, but that's not your responsibility. If you've been faithful to bring these men or women along, then don't be hard on yourself. God may have other plans for them and for you.

Maybe the feedback you get isn't that flattering to you or your leading skills. Sometimes that's going to happen. Relax. There are no perfect group leaders. Some have an easier time than others, but God has given you precisely the gifts he wants you to have. Try to address the problems that are brought up and learn from it. Just don't ignore them. They likely won't go away. Remember ultimately only one vote matters—the Lord's approval for being faithful.

FOR THOUGHT / DISCUSSION

1 What aspects of leading a group do you think will be most natural for you? In what areas might you struggle? How will evaluation help you in both your strong and weak areas?

2 What aspect of leading a group have you seen another do well that you would like to emulate?

3 What are some benefits of involving group members in the evaluation process?

4 What are some possible good reasons to end a group? What are some possible reasons group leaders are often reluctant to bring a group to a conclusion?

149

LAST WEEK, I WAS INVITED TO A FRIEND'S HOME FOR DINNER. WE HADN'T HAD A CHANCE TO SEE EACH OTHER FOR A WHILE, SO I WAS EAGER FOR THE COMPANIONSHIP, AS MUCH AS A GOOD MEAL. WHEN I GOT TO THE DINING ROOM, I WAS EXPECTING TO FIND SOME SORT OF MAIN DISH—PERHAPS A CASSEROLE, OR MAYBE SOME BAKED CHICKEN. I WAS ALSO HOPING FOR A STEAMING DISH OF VEGETABLES AND MAYBE SOME BREAD SERVED IN A BASKET. INSTEAD, SITTING IN THE CENTER OF THE TABLE, WITH ITS JAGGED LID PRIED BACK, WAS A FIVE-POUND CAN OF COLD GREEN BEANS.

"DIG IN!" MY FRIEND SAID. DISGRUNTLED MAY BE TOO STRONG A WORD, BUT I WAS CERTAINLY HOPING FOR MORE. THE BEANS WERE FINE, AND NO DOUBT FULL OF GOOD NUTRIENTS. THE CAN ITSELF WAS STURDY AND CLEARLY LABELED. BUT THE MEAL LACKED A CERTAIN PRESENTATION, NOT TO MENTION FLAVOR.
DON'T GET ME WRONG—I DON'T HAVE ANYTHING AGAINST CANS—THEY DO A GREAT JOB PRESERVING THEIR CONTENTS, AND ENABLING US TO TRANSPORT FOOD ACROSS THOUSANDS OF MILES. IT'S JUST THAT THEY MAKE LOUSY SERVING DISHES.

12

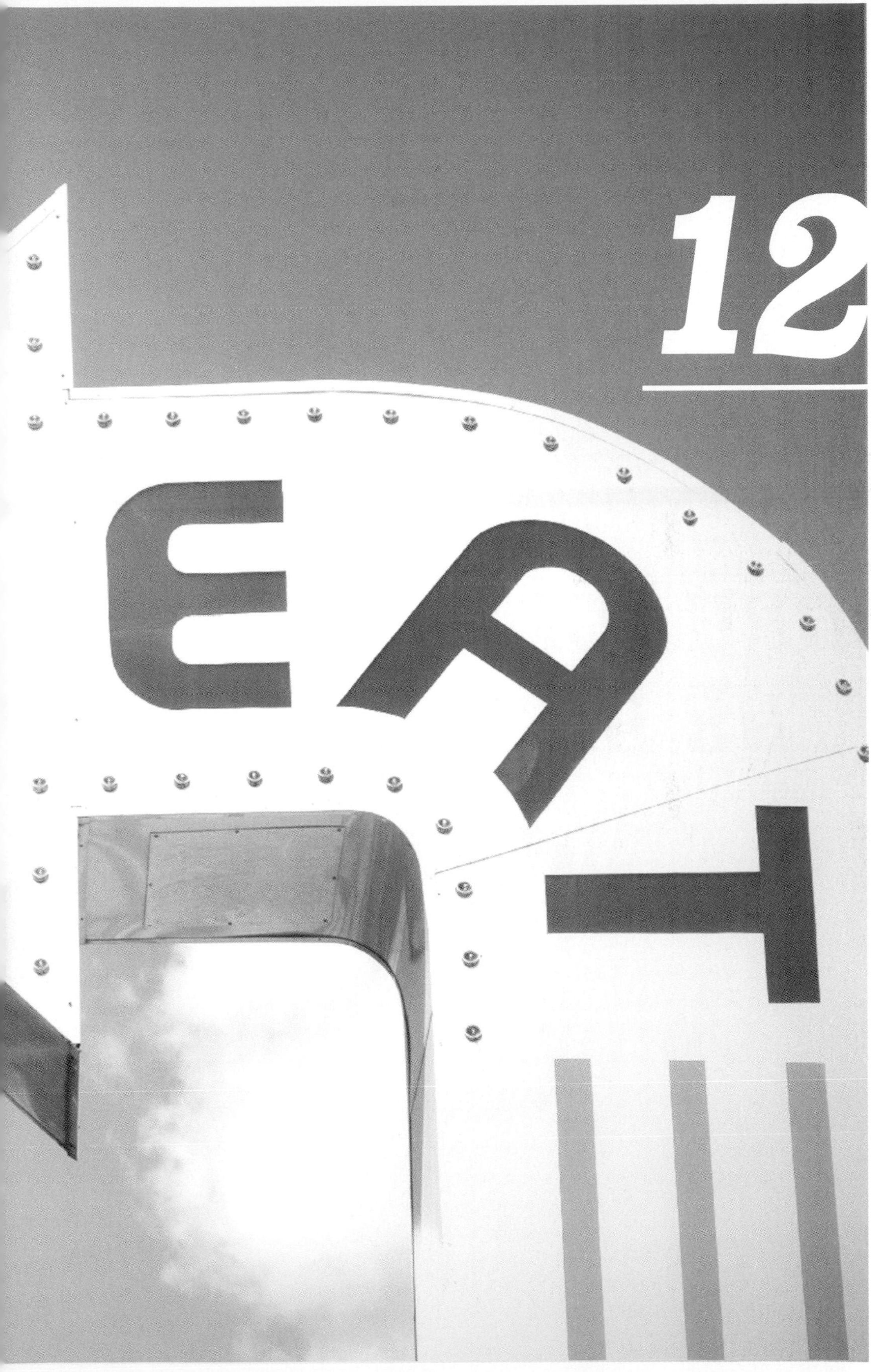

CRU.COMM:
THE BIBLE IN A CAN

12.1 THE ROLE OF CONTENT
12.2 THE DESIGN OF CRU.COMM
12.3 THE EFFECTIVE USE OF CRU.COMM

12.1

THE ROLE OF CONTENT

Now I may not have had an experience exactly like that, but I have had many that are similar. So have a lot of our staff and students. Every week, on campuses across the country, students attend Bible studies that are served right out of the can. This year that "can" may have had the label "Cru.comm" emblazoned on it.

Cru.comm is, unapologetically, Bible study in a can. That is, it is a curriculum of solid biblical data that has been packaged so as to protect its contents from decay, and enable broad distribution. It's not, however, a serving dish. It's the job of the chef (read: Bible study leader), to open up the can, add a little seasoning, and make the meal presentable.

12.2

THE DESIGN OF CRU.COMM

Quality Biblical Content

This book identifies five elements of a healthy small group: quality biblical content, community, richly experiencing Christ, progressive life-change, and outward impact.

Cru.comm is designed to provide you with quality biblical content, with which you can help people understand through a guided process of self-discovered learning, resulting in progressive life-change.

Notice two things in that. First, Cru.comm doesn't even touch on community or outward impact. It's difficult to provide a one-size-fits-all program for community. If each study included a few jokes for you to tell to warm up the group, I can just about guarantee you that they'd flop, and you'd feel like a dork. You can't "can" community.

Similarly, evangelism strategies would likely not fit in with the realities and plans already in place on your campus. It's up to you, locally, to interact with your group, spending time together to build relationships, and to figure out how you can best make the gospel known.

Second, notice where Cru.comm does attempt to resource you. Quality biblical content is what the studies major on. We chose a curriculum of books, and / or passages, that cover topics critical to developing Christ-centered laborers. It has frequently been the case, that our staff and students lead studies on whatever book or topic happens to interest them.

While it's obviously true that all Scripture is profitable, it doesn't necessarily follow that any collection of books, passages, or topics studied, will be equally helpful in producing an effective disciple of Christ—what if, for example, you spent four years slogging through the book of Leviticus? We want to make the best use of the four years we have with our small group, to prepare them for the forty years that will follow. A student, who has learned the material in Cru.comm, over a 3–4 year period, should have developed the worldview that prepares them for a lifetime of ministry.

EVANGELISTIC BIBLE STUDIES

The history of evangelistic Bible studies is a fairly gruesome one: leading questions (e.g. "no one else can forgive sins except who"..."Jesus"), heretical answers, and awkward conversations. Sometimes it can get downright ugly.

Cru.comm includes two evangelistic Bible study series that are about the best content you'll find for generating discussion with a non-Christian audience. The first series deals with issues of the paranormal because these are the spiritual issues non-Christians are talking about. Why not join them in their discussion? The second is a seven-week series on the Seven Deadly Sins.

IN DREAMS
(WHAT DREAMS REVEAL)

5-WEEK TOPICAL DISCUSSION
ON THE PARANORMAL, GOD AND THE BIBLE

Context is Everything

In the creation of Bible study material you can go in one of two directions: study a book of the Bible (a book study) or study biblical topics like prayer, or forgiveness (a topical study). Both are important.

To teach effectively it's essential to isolate and emphasize topics such as prayer or evangelism, yet deep-rooted convictions come from understanding a verse within its biblical context, which mainly happens in the study of a book.

In the making of Cru.comm, a list was made from the complied answers to this question: If a student was involved in a small group for four years, what are the things we would have wanted them to learn? Books of the Bible were then selected that best covered this material. Critical topics, in their critical context: the hope was to accomplish both.

The Level of Maturity

Bible study content needs to be flexible, while at the same time sensitive, to the group's maturity. Cru.comm is divided into four levels of content:

- Exploration Level
- Discovery Level
- Training Group Level
- Action Group Level

While studies can be mixed and matched, thought has been given to maturity and progression ranging from the evangelistic studies of the Exploration Level to principles of leadership discussed in the Action Group Level. Chose content with an eye toward the groups maturity.

155

12.3

THE EFFECTIVE USE OF CRU.COMM

Students will get the most out of a Cru.comm study when the leader is prepared to guide them through a process of self-discovered learning. A leader could just pass out the student notes, ask each question just as it's written, and then read the answers from the key. But it wouldn't be a very engaging study. Rather like a can of cold green beans. It would be far better, if a leader would adequately prepare so as to stimulate the group to discover biblical truths. Below are five tips that may help you do that:

Tips on Preparing for a Cru.comm Study

1 Make sure you understand the material yourself. Read the passage, and the entire guide. Look up parallel texts that are mentioned in the "What do I need to know?" section, as well as cross references or footnotes in your own Bible. Make sure you understand the main point of the study, and how it flows from the text. (This is succinctly stated in "What's the bidg idea?")

But, the best thing you can do, to prepare for any study, is to read and study the rest of your Bible. The broader your knowledge of Scripture, the more insights you are likely to have into any one text. Commit to growing in your knowledge of the Word.

BIBLICAL PROGRESSION
Where possible Cru.comm follows the inspired flow of the biblical context. For example here is the second semester of the Discovery Group Level, all rooted in the gospel of Luke, and following its progression of topics.

1 Follow Me: Commitment
Luke 9:57–62
2 Martha, Martha: Quiet Times
Luke 10:38–42
3 Our Father: Prayer
Luke 11:1–13
4 Beware: Eternal Perspective
Luke 12:1–21
5 Why Worry?: Worry
Luke 12:22–32
6 Last Chance:
God's Kingdom Plan
Luke 12:35–13:35
7 Seeking the Lost: Evangelism
Luke 15:1–32
8 Kingdom Values:
Forgiveness & Thankfulness
Luke 17:1–21
9 A Poor Investment:
Stewardship
Luke 19:11–27

2 Bring your own experiences into the study. It is likely that for every study, there are unmentioned passages of Scripture that are meaningful to you and relevant to the topic at hand. Share those with your group. Perhaps you have an illustration that you find superior to something suggested in the guide. By

all means, do whatever will best help your group learn and discover. You will be a better teacher of the things you are passionate about, and that have been significant to you. In the same spirit, don't be afraid to omit a question that you find unhelpful. You are encouraged to customize, and personalize, the studies.

3 Don't be afraid to teach by making statements. "Self-discovered learning" should not be a euphemism for the pooling of ignorance. We want the students to learn; it's your job to guide them. As such, there will be times every week, where you will need to tell them what they won't otherwise know. In every study, there is information in the "What do I need to know?" section that is not included in the questions. Those represent your chance to be the expert—to teach. In between questions, give some background data, share an illustration, or point them to a parallel text that can give clarity. Some kernels of truth along the way can form the foundations from which the group can make discoveries.

4 At the end of the Study pass out the accompanying article. For most members of your group, covering a biblical topic in exhaustive detail is not amongst the top five reasons for faithful attendance. Consider for example the topic of prayer: how long might a study go that sought to communicate all that the Bible had to say on prayer. For the leader this presents a dilemma: what do you leave out? Difficult decision, but if you've ever sat through a two-hour sermon on Sunday morning you know the horror when no one decides. Almost every study in Cru.comm comes with a compliment article on the topic of discussion to relieve the burden from the study to communicate everything on that topic. If you didn't get to the last three questions, no big deal and no need to run late, the article's got you covered. Just remember to print out one for every group member.

5 Don't pass out the student notes, at least not exactly as they are printed. Heresy, I know, but in my experience, students don't respond well to studies that are over-produced. To that end, the students' notes have a very simple look and feel. But even those, can stifle freedom, and feel too programmatic, so I

prefer not to use them. I'd recommend two options.

It's very easy to copy the content out of the student notes with the text select tool in Acrobat Reader. Then, you can paste the questions into a word processor, cut the ones you don't like, add a few of your own, and personalize it. That way, the notes you pass out are truly your own.

Better still, though, is not to pass out any notes at all. When I lead these studies, I copy the questions I want to use, and comments I wish to make, onto a post-it note or two, that I stick in my Bible. That gives me a structure to follow, but allows greater freedom to follow worthwhile tangents, and enables me to edit on the fly. It makes the studies, in fact and in appearance, more personal and interactive.

By the way, tangents are your friends. They represent the topics about which your students are most interested, engaged, and therefore, best able to learn. If you can engage them with interesting content, they will learn a ton.

APPENDING ARTICLES

Almost every study in Cru.comm comes with a compliment article on the topic of discussion in an attempt to relieve the burden from the Study leader to communicate everything on that topic. The articles were written by a variety of prominent speakers and authors. Here are just a few of the 70+ articles.

- *Let the Nations be Glad, by John Piper*
- *The Example of Humility, by Billy Graham*
- *Partners in Pursuit of Integrity, by Chris Adsit*
- *Run to Win, by Howard Hendricks*
- *Picking Good People, by Henry Cloud*
- *A Parable of the Fishless Fisherman, by John Drescher*
- *Good Old Grace, by Bruce Narramore*
- *Overcoming Tension and Strain, by Oswald Chambers*
- *Use Your Superior Weapons, by Tim Downs*
- *The Holiness of Christ by, Jerry Bridges*
- *How to Witness in the Spirit, by Bill Bright*
- *Tools for Warfare, by Mark Bubeck*
- *The Kingdom Strikes Back, by Ralph Winter*

Application: Progressive Life-Change

The final element of a healthy small group is progressive life-change. In fact, that is the ultimate goal. Our job is not to produce smarter sinners, but to help people be more like Jesus. To that end, make sure you are suggesting a small, practical way, that your small group can begin to apply the lesson of the week.

Each study guide includes application points in the section, "What's our response?" But also be sure to consider how your life has changed over the years. It's very unlikely that you attended a Bible study on generosity, and have been generous ever since. Rather, we learn layer by layer, as the Word of

EVANGELISM TRAINING

A helpful compliment to Cru.comm, for more mature groups, is something called CoJourners. CoJourners is not Bible study material, but contains six to eight-minute segments of evangelism training. CoJourners augments the Bible study with a splash of ministry training; it does not replace it. It keeps the focus of the group from becoming too ingrown, and equips each group member to share Christ with their friends. CoJourner resources are available at CruPress.com.

159

God slowly transforms our minds, and changes our worldview. The most important application of any study, is to be willing to yield yet another area of our lives to the Holy Spirit.

As we study His Word accurately, and assume a humble posture before Him, the real, life-long applications will occur as a matter of course. Make sure your people understand this, so they move toward real maturity, and are not simply jumping through hoops.

CONCLUSION

Cru.comm should be a helpful resource—not to make it easy to lead mediocre studies—but to make it easier to lead great studies that will help us produce Christ-centered laborers.

To purchase Cru.comm call 1.800.827–2788 or go to: CruPress.com. The content is also available online at Centerfieldproductions.com

VICTORY

Well that about wraps up everything you might ever want to know about leading a small group. Perhaps, more than you wanted to know. That's ok... and it's also ok if you forget a great deal of what you've read. We trust that what God wanted you to get out of it, will remain, and this book can also remain, on your shelf that is, as a resource whenever you may need it.

Members of your small group may never know all of the thought, study, prayer and preparation you've put into leading the group. But the real affirmation, encouragement, and victory will be seeing the members of your group thriving in their relationship with Christ and with one another. That's the victory lap.

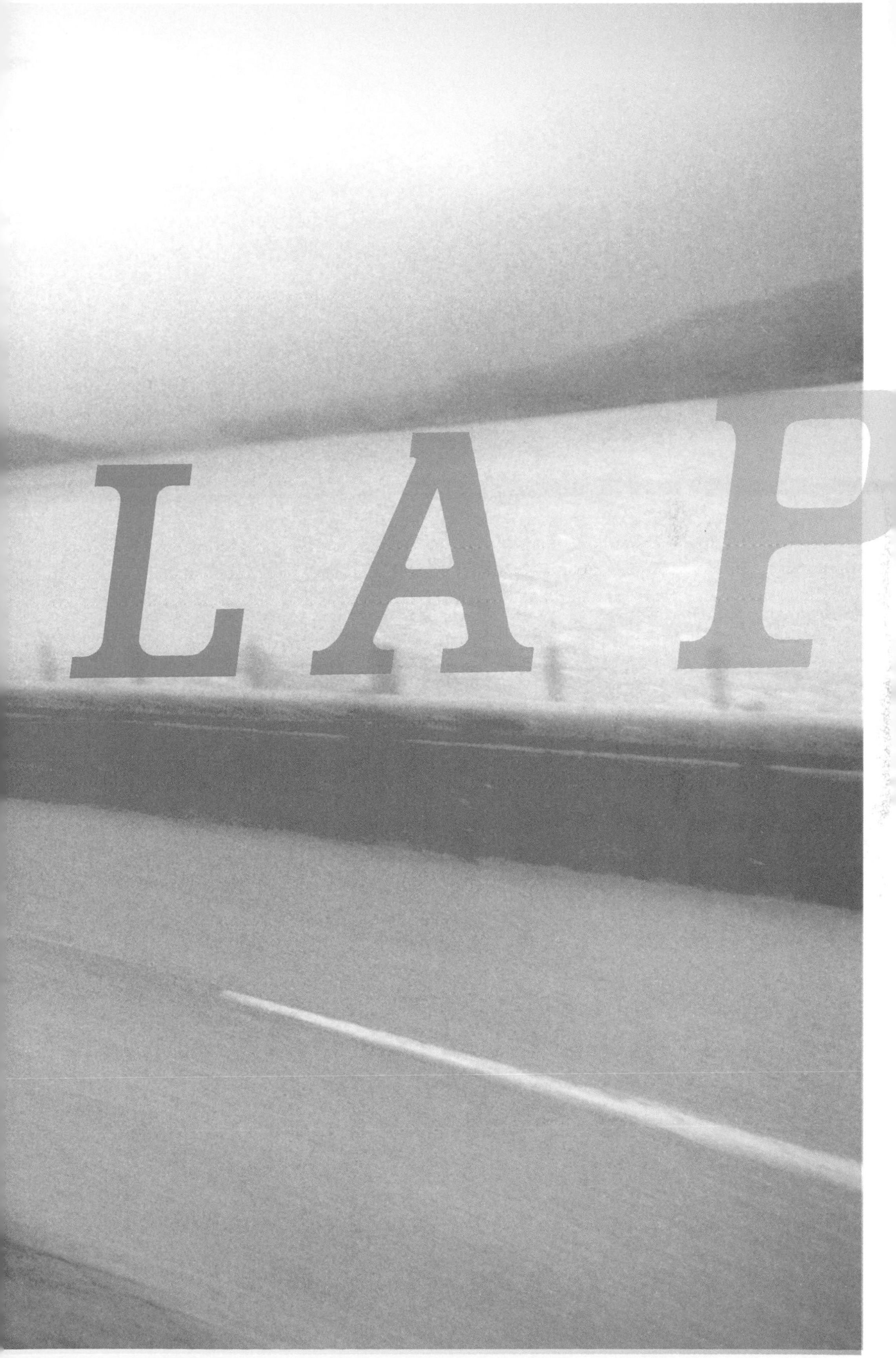
L A P

RESOURCES FOR FURTHER TRAVEL

TEACHING YOUR GROUP TO PRAY

Since this book is about how to lead small groups, there are many other "how to's" we haven't addressed, such as how to have a quiet time, or how to share your faith, or how to study the Bible. But we want to give you some input on how to teach your group to pray, because many groups struggle in this area.

The best way to help your group members learn to pray is to model an enthusiastic heart for prayer. When they see your desire to pray, they'll follow your lead.

Before you get to your small group, pray that God's presence would be evident—that you and those in your group would meet with God and hear from Him.

Establish prayer as a priority during the first few weeks of your small group by simply opening the meeting with prayer and ending by thanking God for what you've learned from your time together.

As your people get to know each other and feel more at ease, have each group member share requests and pray for these, or ask a group member to pray for the group. (Use discretion. Don't put someone on the spot who might be unsure about praying out loud.)

Help your group build their own biblical convictions about the priority of prayer. After going through a Bible study on prayer, set aside time for conversational group prayer. Encourage your group to talk to God and not worry about sounding religious. Explain the "sentence prayers" concept of praying a short sentence of praise or petition.

Then begin setting aside time each week during your small group for prayer. Here are a few ideas:

- Have a specific focus for your prayer time and alternate it each week—i.e., personal requests, unsaved friends, application of what was studied from the Word, a thanksgiving and praise time, ministry outreach events, etc.

- Copy or download brief segments from news reports, current programs and talk shows that are related to issues you're praying about. Start your prayer time with these clips.

- Share testimonies of ways God has answered prayer or what God is teaching each person.

- Help your group begin to keep a journal. Have everyone write a page about their day, what they've learned from God, and how they feel about what's going on in their lives. Then pray together over the needs revealed.

- Write a private love letter to God to begin a time of praise.

- Keep a small group prayer notebook of your specific prayer requests and the date of the answers.

- Praise God together: listen to praise music, sing with praise music or guitar.

- Go to locations of upcoming events, outreaches or target areas and take "Jericho Walks" (Joshua 6). Pray in pairs walking around (or just walking by) the location. You may choose to walk around the area once or follow the pattern set up for Joshua and the Israelites—walk around the area praying once for six days and then on the seventh day walk around it seven times while praying.

- Read aloud written prayers, songs or interesting quotes found in liturgical books, hymnals and Christian books (suggested authors: E.M. Bounds, Richard Foster, C.S. Lewis, Oswald Chambers).

- Read and pray through a passage like Psalm 136 or one of Paul's prayers (Ephesians 1:18-20; Philippians 1:9-11). There are plenty of other Scripture verses and prayers you can pray through.

- Read through a book on prayer together; discuss and apply the principles you glean from it. A book to consider is *Fireseeds of Spiritual Awakening* by Dan Hayes (Crupress.com).

As your group develops a Christ-dependent, prayerful lifestyle, continue to encourage them in prayer and accountability by dividing the small group into prayer partners. Encourage them to pray together and for each other in their private prayer times.

Remember that it takes time for a group to feel comfortable praying together. It also takes time to cultivate and develop a heart for prayer. So, use some of these ideas to move your group to the next step in their prayer life.

NEW ADVENTURES FOR VETERAN GROUPS

165

OK, your group is coming together and you want to try something new and adventurous that is appropriate for your maturing group. Here are a few ideas, although there are a lot more that you could come up with on your own:

- Sing hymns or praise songs together (a cappella or with a tape).

- Read worshipful passages from the Bible (Psalms for example) and pray them back to the Lord.

- Write a letter of praise to God.

- Study a book on the attributes of God such as *Knowing God* by J.I. Packer, or *Knowledge of the Holy* by A.W. Tozer. Also, quite helpful is the section on the character and attributes of God in *Systematic Theology* by Wayne Grudem.

- Go somewhere and build an altar to the Lord. This can be as simple as a pile of rocks. Group members can toss in a rock for each specific thing they are grateful for or ways they've seen God work. If the group stays together for awhile, return to the place and make a tradition of reflecting on all God has done and add to the pile (see Joshua 4).

- Memorize Scripture together. You can have each person recite what they've learned the past week, or have some group goals. You can choose topical issues for memorization, such as the character of God, or you can choose a paragraph, chapter, or book of the Bible to memorize.

- Teach your group members how to study the Word for themselves. If you don't know how to do this, ask your Campus Crusade director for a person who could help. Some books you might find helpful are *Living by the Book*, by Howard and William Hendricks (Moody Press) and *Guide to Understanding Your Bible* by Josh McDowell (Thomas Nelson).

- Assign each person a prayer partner.

- Begin to share more personal information about your spiritual life.

- Attend a retreat or a conference as a group, or plan your own weekend getaway.

- Structure fellowship time within the group to expose needs, then others in the group can help in these areas. For example, have group members share one area of their life that could be stronger with the benefit of another person's help.

- Write encouragement cards to one another at the end of a semester or year to celebrate your time together and what God has done.

- Have people pair up to have devotionals together every once in a while.

- Bring in someone who has been on an overseas project to share about their experience.

- Pray for unreached peoples. You might find *Operation World* by Patrick Johnston (Zondervan) helpful.

- Have a "world vision" time in your group on a regular basis. Have someone report on a part of the world, a missionary, or what God is doing overseas.

- Read books on world missions. For example, *From Jerusalem to Irian Jira* by Ruth Tucker is an excellent book of missionary biographies.

- Give money to help overseas missionaries.

- Do an evangelistic event as a group that targets international students, such as showing the "JESUS" film, having an international dinner, or befriending an international student.

- Teach them how to share their faith and then take them with you to do it.

- Teach them how to disciple others and help them get started.

- Share your testimony, teach them how to prepare their own, and then give them a chance to share it.

- Encourage them to come to Campus Crusade meetings that teach them how to effectively share their faith.

SAMPLE PURPOSE & CONTENT WORKSHEET

A worksheet like this is helpful when first planning for your group. It can also serve as a helpful reminder to be sure you stay on course. Chapter 4 discusses how to use this sheet.

167

1 After prayerfully assessing the needs of my group members, I think their basic spiritual needs are:

I think their basic felt needs are:

2 In light of their needs and the overall purpose of our campus ministry, the purpose of my group will be:

3 This purpose is best accomplished by meeting this many weeks:

4 I think the best topics to fulfill the purpose of our group are:

5 I will pray God changes the lives of those in my group in these ways:

SAMPLE SMALL GROUP NEEDS SURVEY

A survey like this helps you discover the needs of those in your group. Usually it's given at the beginning of the group. Because it takes some time to complete, it's best to have people give them back to you at a later time.

Give me your input on the small group. I want our group to be beneficial to everyone in it.

1 What would you like to get out of this small group? Why?

2 What topics would you like to study that would most help you grow in your relationship with God?

3 What frustrates you most as you try to live the Christian life?

4 How has the campus environment influenced your faith?

5 Are there any issues that have come up on campus that you feel threaten your Christian faith? If so, what are they?

6 Summarize your Christian experience in three or four brief sentences. Try to include the highs and lows, whatever seems most significant.

7 In general, how confident are you in your knowledge of the Bible? What, specifically, would you like to learn about God's Word?

8 The one or two things God could ask you to do that you wouldn't want to do are _____. Why do you feel this way?

9 Do you prefer large or small groups?

10 Do you have a job? If so, how many hours a week do you work?

11 What TV shows do you watch regularly?

12. Are you involved in any clubs or politics on campus? If so, which ones?

13 When learning something, do you learn best by:

    a) talking it through.

    b) having it explained to you.

    c) having it demonstrated or illustrated.

14 What do you value most in a leader?

    a) competency

    b) caring and compassion

    c) structure

    d) flexibility

    e) honesty

    f) belief in me

    g) other: _____

15 What do you need the most from a leader?

    a) specific direction

    b) honesty

    c) encouragement

    d) patience

    e) a shove

    f) other: _____

16 Is there anything else you'd like to say about our small group:

SAMPLE SMALL GROUP MEETING EVALUATION

It's good to think through each group session after it is over. Here are some questions you might ask regarding the group. Don't let these put you under the pile. Virtually no one fills out a sheet like this after every group. Use what you find helpful from it.

1 Did you think/feel the small group meeting was successful? Why?

2 Was everyone at the meeting who should have been there? What do you need to do to contact those who were absent?

3 Did you begin and end on time? What do you need to do to improve on this?

4 Were you thoroughly prepared for the session? What would enable you to be better prepared next time?

5 What was your purpose for this particular lesson? After the group did you feel you met your objectives?

6 How is the sense of community within the group? What might help improve this?

7 Did you feel like you understood the biblical passage? What could you have done to be more prepared in God's Word?

8 Did everyone participate in the discussion? Did certain people tend to dominate

or be left out of the discussion? What can be done to help people feel included?

9 Did your questions and learning activities help members discover the truth of God's Word for themselves? How could these have been better?

10 Did the group get off on too many tangents? How can you keep the discussion on target?

11 Did the lesson meet specific needs in students' lives? How could you have made it more practical?

171

12 Did you share specifically how God is changing you?

13 Did members leave with a concrete plan of application?

14 Are there people in the group that you should meet with personally before the next session?

15 How is the group doing in turning the corner from getting to giving?

In light of my answers to the above questions, I will make the following two changes for the next group meeting:

These areas are going well so I will keep the following things the same:

SAMPLE SMALL GROUP MEMBERS' EVALUATION

An evaluation like this could be taken halfway through a group to make mid-course corrections. It is short enough to take during the group time. Chapter 11 gives you ideas on evaluation.

1 I look forward to coming to this small group: Yes / No / Sometimes. Why?

2 I benefit from this time: Yes / No / Sometimes.
  For example:

3 I wish we would do the following:

4 I feel a part of the discussion during the group time: Yes / No. Why?

5 Other comments or suggestions:

ORDERING CRU.COMM

The contents of Chapter 12 dealt with the small group material Cru.comm. To order, call 1.800.827–2788 or go to: CruPress.com.

ORDERING THE COMPASS

The Compass follows the same format as Cru.comm but contains over 40 personal discipleship appointments. To order, call 1.800.827–2788 or go to: CruPress.com.

The content of Cru.comm and the Compass is also available online at center-fieldproductions.com.

ORDERING THE COJOURNERS EQUIPPING PACK

The CoJourners Equipping Pack contains six to eight minute training sessions for use in small groups. To order, call 1.800.827–2788 or go to: CruPress.com.

Chapter One Notes

174

Chapter Two Notes

Chapter Three Notes

175

Chapter Four Notes

Chapter Five Notes

Chapter Six Notes

Chapter Seven Notes

Chapter Eight Notes

Chapter Nine Notes

Chapter Ten Notes

Chapter Eleven Notes

Chapter Twelve Notes